Mothers, Sisters, Daughters

STANDING ON THEIR SHOULDERS

Blessings!

EDWINA GATELEY

AND

SANDRA MATTUCCI

ORBIS BOOKS

Maryknoll, New York 10545

Second printing, April 2014

Founded in 1970, Orbis Books endeavors to publish works that enlighten the mind, nourish the spirit, and challenge the conscience. The publishing arm of the Maryknoll Fathers and Brothers, Orbis seeks to explore the global dimensions of the Christian faith and mission, to invite dialogue with diverse cultures and religious traditions, and to serve the cause of reconciliation and peace. The books published reflect the views of their authors and do not represent the official position of the Maryknoll Society. To learn more about Maryknoll and Orbis Books, please visit our website at www.maryknollsociety.org.

Library of Congress Cataloging-in-Publication Data

Gateley, Edwina.
  Mothers, sisters, daughters : standing on their shoulders / Edwina Gateley and Sandra Mattucci.
      p. cm.
  ISBN 978-1-57075-950-5 (pbk.)
  1. Women in Christianity--Biography. 2. Women and religion--Biography. 3. Women--Biography. 4. Courage. I. Title.
  BR1713.G38 2012
  270.092'52--dc23
                                        2011029100

*In memory of my mother
on whose shoulders I stand.*

*Also for my sister, Maureen,
for her many years of devoted caregiving.*

*And for Vena, whose hospitality and labor,
so freely given, is a credit to St. Benedict.*

*And for Connie, OSB, who burned a thousand
candles on my behalf.*

—Edwina Gateley

*I am grateful to all my soul sisters and soul brothers who
have awakened in my heart, through their presence in my life,
a deeper appreciation for "connectedness." For those whom I
yet have not met, I await to embrace in the larger circle of
creation's dance.*

*I acknowledge Sister Alberta Surowiec, fssj, for her
unwavering support of me as I sketched the portraits and wrote
the biographies and for the time she spent in editing my work,*

*Edwina Gateley who opened to me the lives of these amazing
women and let me stand on their shoulders beside her,*

*and Michael Leach for his support, encouragement, and
belief in me and this book's unfolding.*

—Sandra Mattucci

Acknowledgments

In gratitude to Sister Monique Gautier, CSJ, who spent many hours
typing and editing the manuscript for this book.

Contents

INTRODUCTION

Mothers, Sisters, Daughters: Standing on Their Shoulders had its beginnings on a retreat I was leading during which we explored the stories of significant women who had made a difference in the world. Their struggles, joys, dreams, and achievements were a source of enormous encouragement and empowerment to the participants. Half way through the retreat Sandra Mattucci, an artist, shared with me sketches she had drawn of some of the women about whom I was speaking. I was very impressed—and so were all the other women at the gathering!

They wanted more of both! Out of that came this book of my stories and Sandy's narratives and sketches.

It would be, and is, a source of information for women to get in touch with the stories of those who have gone before us and whose courage and determination serve as an inspiration for contemporary women.

"Mothers, Sisters, Daughters" tells of twenty-two women from different parts of the world—politicians, mystics, religious women, poets, women from Scripture, environmentalists, and more. Some of the women are well known, others are total strangers. What gives them a place in this book is that in their own different ways each brought some light into our world. Many had dreams and the determination and courage to follow them—in some cases leading to their deaths. Others led amazing and exemplary lives or were heroic because of their faithful and unswerving commitment to do what they believed was right—no matter what the risk or consequences.

We are all connected to every living creature—even to those long dead. For the most part we are not conscious of this invisible thread of connection. Traditionally the church calls it "the communion of saints."

Saints or sinners—we are all part of this web of being. When we pray to the saints, beg intercession from dead family members or friends, or storm the heavens for assistance on earth, we are participating in this mystery of connectedness.

It follows (at least to me!) that we are capable of tapping into the energy of individuals who have gone before us. Whether this is real or imaginary does not matter. What does matter is that we can be, and often are, encouraged, inspired, and affected by great souls—living or dead.

This book is about great souls. May they assist us on our own stumbling journeys to God.

Edwina Gateley

Mother
(1910 – 2010)

Catherine (Rene) Pye Gateley was born outside the ancient Roman city of Lancaster, England, in the rural village of Bayhorse. She was born into the simple lifestyle of a farming community in the country—long before any of our modern technologies existed.

Rene's ambition was to become a teacher but that kind of education was hard come by in the 1930s, and she never reached college level. She did, however, have a passion for music and became an accomplished pianist, finding expression for her musical talent as the church organist at Sunday services for the larger part of her adult life.

She married John Christopher Gateley, an Irishman, during the early years of World War II, and they had three children, including the author of this book, Edwina. A time of great poverty for many families, Rene struggled to raise her children and earn a living while her husband was away at war. As a bus conductress on the city buses, Rene worked twelve hours a day, six days a week, for over thirty years until her retirement, selling tickets and traveling all over the area. A popular and well-loved employee, Rene worked long and hard to provide for her family.

Rene's faith in God, simplicity, basic goodness, and amazing sense of humor endeared her to all. In spite of poverty and hardship, she lived life to the fullest. She was never ill, never took any medicines, was never hospitalized, never showed any anger, and never complained. Dying two weeks after her one hundredth birthday she had indeed lived a full life.

~

No one really knew you, Mum.
They knew me, of course.
I have traveled the world.
Written books.
Spoken to thousands.
My name is recognized.
My work applauded.
But no one recognized
or applauded you.

Outside the little town
where you lived for 100 years,
you were simply unknown,
walking your path
in gentle, quiet faithfulness.
Nothing great or momentous,
just everyday living
fulfilled with beauty, grace,
and goodness.

You did not address crowds
as I do,

but you watched
the setting of the sun
in awe and amazement,
declaring to the empty room:
"How beautiful! How beautiful!
Thank you, God!"
Your soul was seized and held
by the ordinary miracles
of life and nature all around you.
And, like a child,
you shone with the delight
of it all.

Oh, no,
you did not write or sell books
as I do.
You spent your life
selling bus tickets
to folks who had no cars
and, like you,
traveled by bus or bike.
But every ticket sold,
every simple transaction,
brought with it
human goodness and laughter.

The bus folks
loved you, Mum.
They recognized your simplicity,
your deep goodness,
and your authentic joy in life.

MOTHERS, SISTERS, DAUGHTERS

You didn't do anything
great or momentous.
But like so many other
unknown mothers,
you baked and cooked
and cleaned and laundered
with a dedication and devotion
way beyond
many mighty achievements
of stars and celebrities.
Your star
did not shine illustrious.
But it was always there,
steady and sure,
a constant, comforting presence
in the pressure and chaos
of my own wild life.
You were always there
for all of us,
and we took your presence
for granted
as we rushed in
to greet you
and then left to go about
our vital business,
leaving you waving frantically
with tears in your eyes.

But you waited, still, at the door
with your teapot and your love.

For 100 years you were there
with your eternal welcome,
eyes shining in joy and surprise
(though you knew I was coming).

You'd have thought
I was an angel
sent by God:
"Is that you?
"Is that you?"
And you would simply stand,
transfixed,
gazing with delight
at the prodigal daughter
come home.
No god
could have been
so joyous in welcome.

I miss you, Mum,
beautiful soul.
I need no saints,
nor martyrs and virgins
to tell me of God—
only you, Mum,
with your teapot and your love
standing in the doorway,
shining with delight:
"Is it you, Edwina?
Oh, is it you?"

Hildegard of Bingen
(1098–1179)

Hildegard, a Benedictine nun and one of the most important figures of the Middle Ages, has been described as "the greatest woman of her time." When she was ten years old her father, a knight, sent her to a Benedictine monastery to be educated. At eighteen she became a nun and eventually Abbess of her community.

Hildegard's gifts and achievements were prodigious. She was musician, composer, scientist, doctor, artist, writer, mystic, and visionary. She was also gifted with the prophetic insight that led her to declare that the earth and the environment must not be harmed, clearly by future generations. Care for the earth and church reform were major themes in her art and writing.

Hildegard experienced a series of powerful visions that she expressed in both art and writing. The Inquisition questioned the authenticity of her visions and Hildegard was subject to an ecclesiastical trial that ultimately vindicated her. An outspoken critic of church corruption and abuse, Hildegard wrote frequently to the Pope urging him to work harder for church reform. A strong and independent-minded woman, she clashed with her Abbot when she buried a young, excommunicated crusader in the monastery grounds. Ordered to exhume his body, Hildegard refused, and as a punishment she and her community were forbidden to sing the Divine Office and were barred from receiving Communion. Hildegard took to her bed in depression for six months. It was towards the end of that time that she experienced her powerful visions. She and her sisters left the abbey, and Hildegard built her own monastery across the Rhine.

Hildegard wrote nine books, seventy-seven hymns, and seventy poems. She described herself as "a feather on the breath of God." She was truly a remarkable and prophetic woman.

The earth must not be harmed.
The earth must not be destroyed.

How could it be,
Hildegard of Bingen, woman of God,
that nearly a 1000 years ago
you had the vision and insight
to utter words that speak to us
so powerfully today,
now in the 21st century?
Ah, Hildegard,
were you so saturated
with the grace of God
that it thrust you through the centuries
to see, in pain and horror,

the planet we now inhabit?
Did you see,
in your nightly visions,
the oil spills,
the toxic waste,
the polluted waters,
the myriad habitat loss,
and the ravaged earth?
Did your soul weep for us
so long ago,
Hildegard, woman of God?
And will you weep with us today
as we come, oh, so slowly,
to acknowledge and echo your words:
The earth must not be harmed.
The earth must not be destroyed.

Oh, are we now humble
and broken enough, Hildegard,
to embrace and proclaim
your understanding that
if feminine soul life
were restricted and repressed,
all life would be affected
and eventually
dry up?

Are we drying up, Hildegard?
Are the juices of God's grace

no longer flowing freely within us
like a river that should water
dry and desert places?

And are we no longer
feeding the hungry?
clothing the naked?
housing the homeless ?
giving water to the thirsty?
Oh, we hear you, Hildegard!
We hear you now, woman of God,
and we weep for our blindness
and our lack of vision.
We lament
that your prophecies and pleadings
fell upon deaf ears,
though you never hesitated, Hildegard,
to declare the truth of your visions.

You, who declared yourself
a feather on the breath of God,
were not afraid
to speak aloud
to the church of your time,
condemning corruption, power,
and sexual abuse
and calling for
repentance, reform, and accountability.
Indeed, a prophet also
for our church today!

Perhaps that is why so few
know of you, Hildegard—
your words and visions
were a threat to the status quo.
Your gifts
were many and powerful—
healer, musician, prophet,
visionary, artist, scientist, doctor,
mystic, and rebel—
and female to boot!
Why are we surprised
that your voice was silenced
over the centuries?

Why are we surprised
that you were such a threat
to a corrupt male hierarchy
in a church that had lost its way
and is still, today,
wandering?

But your voice,
God driven,
and your admonition:
"Wake up!"
echoes through the centuries
and is heard now
by our listening ears,
attuned nearly 1000 years on
to your passionate voice

calling for healing and new life.
We hear you,
Hildegard, woman of God!
We hear your plea
for balance in relationship
with all living things,
with the earth,
the cosmos, and
all of creation.
We hear your call
for the feminine
to rise up in compassion
to bring healing to
our broken world.

Ah, Hildegard, woman of God,
may your music
and your prophetic vision
touch our souls today
as we come to understand
how the Word and Grace of God
speak to us through the ages,
again and again and again,
calling us to awaken to the healing power
that resides within all of us.

No matter how broken,
no matter how sinful,
no matter how wounded,

this healing power,
eternal and endless,
waits to burst upon us
with its bountiful
and extravagant promise
of new life.
And God,
ever longing,
waits for us tirelessly,
century after century,
to hear the urgent whisper:
The earth must not be harmed.
The earth must not be destroyed.

Oh, pray for us,
Hildegard, woman of God,
Pray for us!

Miriam
(Exodus 2:1-4)

According to the Book of Exodus, Miriam saved the life of her baby brother, Moses, and became a significant leader of the People of Israel during the time of the Exodus from Egypt. Fearful for the safety of the infant Moses, Miriam and her mother placed him in a basket in the river. Miriam waited and watched until the daughter of Pharaoh came to bathe and found and rescued the baby. Miriam, her mother, and Pharaoh's daughter, without realizing it, were instruments of God's salvific plan for the People of Israel. Moses would later be called to lead the people out of enslavement in Egypt, and it was Miriam who went before them dancing and playing her tambourine!

Miriam has been named the first woman in scripture to be given the recognition of prophetess. She had prophesied that her parents would give birth to a child who would bring about redemption. During the flight from Egypt, Miriam was leader of song and dance and, according to tradition, was instrumental in guiding the people to a well, providing water for them in the desert.

The story of Miriam is one of trust in God's providence. Even though her feet never touched the ground of the Promised Land, and even when she was stricken with Tzaars (an affliction generally translated as leprosy), Miriam maintained her place as well-loved prophet and leader amongst the People of Israel.

> Stealthily, silently she stole down
> to the riverbank—
> a mother in anguish,
> clutching child
> so newly slipped
> from the waters of her womb.
> And there,
> washed in her tears
> and embraced
> by desperate prayers for survival,
> she placed him
> into the hands of God
> upon the treacherous waters of the Nile.
>
> In the shadows, hiding,
> watching, waiting,
> hovered Miriam, his sister,
> expectant of miracle,
> daring deliverance
> from the Other Side,
> dreaming of, and demanding,
> complicity and salvation
> from the death dealer's
> daughter.
> Hush, she comes,

the other woman,
death dealer's daughter—
privileged, rich, and distinguished,
not poor, dispossessed, and desperate
like Miriam and her mother.
But she pauses,
sees the child—
fragile, innocent, vulnerable—
and in that moment of recognition,
all difference dissolves,
all separateness melts,
death is defied
in the glance of compassion.
The other woman
becomes mother,
sister, and daughter,
linked by love,
the three
are one.
In silent conspiracy meeting at the water,
defying death,
the women come together,
to bring about new life.
Miriam,
brave mediator of the older women
brings them together
in nurturing and motherhood.
Surrogate and mother
assume new roles,
seeking alternative ways,

weaving different threads together,
crossing the boundaries of class and race,
so that life might triumph
over death.
Bold brave Miriam!
You knew from early age
the essential solidarity
of the feminine
in the journey of life.
But afterwards,
your story
is shrouded in silence, Miriam,
brave sister of Moses,
as the brother you helped to save
rose up
in power and authority and leadership.
We, your sisters, know
about that reality.
For still today,
in church and state and all forms
of governance,
our brothers rise and rule
whilst we women
conspire together
to nurture, feed, heal, and serve.
There would be no life
without us, Miriam.
Our wisdom and compassion
conspire still
to defy the death dealers.

We march against war
in the midst of war.
We cry out for peace
in places of violence.

Today our voices (once whispers)
are rising louder
for alternative forms of
leadership and a different use of power—
for consensus—not infallibility,
for equality—not racism,
for compassion—not retribution.
We are standing up, Miriam,
as you did,
for life.
We are demanding that our resources
be shared,
that our weapons be put down,
that our waters be cleaned,
our air protected,
and the earth be honored.
We are standing, Miriam,
for our sisters—the waters,
for our brothers—the forests,
for our mother—the earth.
We women are standing together, Miriam,
for life and for survival
in our generation.
And we celebrate that, Miriam!
We celebrate our call to leadership
as you did,

when at last you re-emerged
in the story of your people's journey
to freedom.
From the waters of the sea
you rose again before us,
dancing and singing with tambourine,
and the women followed
your leadership,
declaring you Prophet!
as you led them
into freedom, singing.

Ah! You danced
in joy and gratitude,
personifying the deepest form
of prayer and worship.
Miriam!
First woman in all of Israel
to be called
Prophet.
Ah—leader of God's people—
you entered fully
into the dance of life!
Ever defiant of oppression,
at the banks of the river
and the shore of the sea,
you embraced, Miriam,
all the chaos of life.
In words of faith and deliverance
you sang the song of praise

that later
(the scholars tell us)
was stolen and placed
in the mouth of Moses, your brother—
myth,
not reality,
claiming religious leadership and worship
as the province of the male.
It was then in the wilderness,
traditional place of struggle and dissent,
that along with your brother Aaron,
you challenged
the singular leadership of Moses,
declaring that God spoke also
through you—
the woman.
Ah, Miriam!
You paid then
the price of prophetic voice!
Punished (it would seem)
for your daring and your protest,
you were struck down by
leprous disease.
(Not so your brother, Aaron—
it was you, the woman,
who was punished and condemned.)
We know of that too.
In our times also, Miriam,
we women are harassed, labeled,
imprisoned, burned, and stoned

for infringements
of patriarchal codes and laws
while our brothers are exempt.
You too, became reject and outcast.
You, who saved
by evading and defying the code of law
were sacrificed yourself
by those very same codes.
But even as you were excluded
and marginalized—
forever now impure—
the people—your people—
refused to continue their journey
until you returned to them,
until you walked again
with them,
continuing the journey together.

Your voice is never heard again, Miriam,
but such loyalty and devotion
begs the question,
Who indeed,
led the people toward liberation?
At your death
all the waters of the desert dried up.
You, Miriam,
who gave life at the water's edge,
You, Miriam,
who celebrated life at the shores of the sea,
are mourned now by nature

as the waters of life—
the symbols of your leadership—
disappear at your death
into the wilderness.

Ah, Miriam,
archetype of female prophetic leadership,
we your sisters, mothers, and daughters
gather in your memory.

We honor you, Miriam,
we celebrate you
at the waters of life,
and we shall stand, brave and strong,
singing our song
to you, Miriam,
prophet and leader.

We stand on your shoulders,
Soul Sister.

Annalena Tonelli
(1943–2003)

A nnalena found her deepest fulfillment in becoming one with the poor.

Born April 2, 1943, Annalena grew up in Forli, Romagna, Italy. From her early childhood years, this Italian, Roman Catholic woman chose a life lived for others.

She worked as a volunteer in Africa for thirty-three years. She wanted to serve the poor, the suffering, and the abandoned and desired only to follow Christ. Nothing interested her more than Christ and the poor who lived in Him.

Annalena lived a life of *radical poverty*. She had a PhD in law, but sought avenues that allowed her to minister in the health services arena. In 1969, she went to Africa. Qualified to teach English, she worked in Kenyan Secondary Schools and was also a high school teacher in Wajir (a semi-desert region in northeast Kenya) where Somali persons (nomadic) dwelt. It was there that Annalena truly began her work, supported by the Committee Against World Hunger of Forli, which she had helped to establish.

Annalena lived without a salary and never gave thought to

creating a pension plan that would support her during her senior years. She worked independently, raising the funds ($20,000 a month) to run a 200-bed tuberculosis hospital in Borama. Annalena earned certificates/diplomas in tropical medicines, community medicines, tuberculosis control, and control of leprosy so as to better care for the people she loved and served. In 1976, she was responsible for a World Health Organization (WHO) project that treated nomadic persons with tuberculosis.

In 1984, amid political and inter-clan clashes, Annalena was forced to leave Kenya. Annalena had helped prevent countless killings, but having been in danger many times—kidnapped, beaten, and her life threatened—she had no other option but to leave.

Annalena went to Somalia, where her works included a hospital; a school for special education for deaf, blind, and disabled children; a program for the eradication of female genital mutilation; cure and prevention of HIV/AIDS; and aid for outcasts, poor, and orphans. Annalena's care for refugees earned her the Nanasen Refugee Award in 2003, presented by the United Nations High Commissioner for Refugees, as recognition for her unrelenting service.

Annalena Tonelli's life was tragically ended in 2003 when she was assassinated by gunmen in Borama in the tuberculosis hospital that she had established.

Annalena never saw her life as "sacrifice." In her own words, "There is no sacrifice. It's pure happiness. Who else on earth has such a beautiful life?"

~

Why aren't you famous, Annalena?
Why doesn't the world know
of your life of amazing love,
courage, and holiness?
Why doesn't the church
preach your name,
declare your virtues,
and acknowledge that you,
devout Catholic laywoman,
gave your life
to the most destitute and forgotten
until you were shot
and martyred for your love?

Your hidden story is a treasure.
It is too beautiful,
too awesome,
and almost too amazing
to be believed.

For over 30 years
you lived in destitution
amongst the Muslim nomads
of parched Somalia.
In love with God
and God's poorest,
you made your home
amongst them,
responding with creativity
and imagination

to every desperate need
that rose up
before your door.
"Life has meaning only
if one loves," you whispered.
And the poor heard—
gathering in longing,
they came to you—
the diseased,
the dying,
the deaf,
the blind,
the hungry,
the rejected.
And all were welcome.
All were loved.
All became your family,
living together
in total poverty and love.

While the world ate and drank
and went about its business
of building and succeeding,
fighting and loving,
shopping and dreaming,
you lived on the edges,
unknown, unseen, unheralded,
driven by love
into sick and dirty places
under the hot desert sun.

We didn't see you, Annalena!
You were too far away,
too isolated,
too alone
to be noticed.
But your works rose up
wondrous
in the wilderness—
hospitals, schools, clinics,
and even a makeshift mosque
for the Muslim people
whom you served.
Moved by the powerful commitment
of your Christian faith,
baffled by your celibacy
and your passionate devotion
to Christ,
your Muslim community
honored your lone witness
and the light it left around you,
Annalena.
"Faith without love is useless,"
you declared,
"Everything is grace."
But for love and grace
you endured
death threats, beatings, and
the violence of tribal warfare.
Dreaming of heaven

you often lived through hell—
and endured it.

Burying the massacred dead,
tending the dying,
you risked your life
whilst daring to declare,
"All is grace."

Discipleship gone mad . . .

In you, Annalena,
Christianity and Islam
came together
in mutual respect and admiration.

In you, Annalena,
God lived and shone
in the wilderness.

In you, Annalena,
Jesus rose again—
healing, teaching, tending—
making all things one.
You lived "waiting for God" and
with your murder,
brave and holy woman,
the Cross
was raised again,
and we have an unsung saint,

another woman, to remind us
in our dim seeing
of the brilliance and beauty
of love.

May we all be one . . .

The Woman at the Well
(John 4:1-30)

Traveling from Jerusalem to Galilee, Jesus entered Samaria. Samaria was a place that most Jews deliberately avoided. Jews and Samaritans were basically enemies, having nothing to do with each other and having different locales for worship.

In the heat of the afternoon Jesus, tired and thirsty, stopped to rest. He sat by a well while his disciples went off to find some food. As noon approached, a stranger—a woman—came to the well to fill her water jug. The timing was wrong—women did not go to the well in the heat of the noonday sun! It was an activity that was almost always done at sunrise or sunset when it was cool. It was also a social activity—women walked together to chat and catch up with their news. The fact that the Samaritan woman arrived alone and at the wrong time leads us to believe that she was something of an outcast amongst her people and had to avoid the company of other women. Later in conversation with Jesus, it became clear that there had been many men in her life. One could reasonably surmise that the woman was the village prostitute.

Jesus broke the cultural taboo by speaking to her (Jews did not speak to Samaritans). He not only spoke to her, he asked her for a favor—for water! The woman was stunned and could not believe that a man—a Jew—would ask her for a drink! Jesus then offered her Living Water. He told her about her own life, and she recognized him as a prophet.

The encounter became a moment of conversion and joy for the woman who then proclaimed Jesus as Messiah. She believed in the Water of Life that Jesus offered her and was so filled with joy that she ran back to her village proclaiming the Good News! She became the first evangelist!

I am glad it is so hot,
for now I can be sure
that no other woman
will endure this heat
to come to the well.
Good. I will be alone.
But I must hurry
while the village is
still sleeping in the
noonday heat.
I must not be seen.
They don't want
to run into me—
a prostitute—the village harlot!
They treat me
like I am diseased,
like I am dirty.

I don't care . . .
But I am so thirsty . . .
I need water . . .
Water . . .
so refreshing, so cool,
it makes even me
feel clean!
There is the well—
just ahead.
Not much further.
I am so thirsty.

But there is someone already there!
Sitting on the edge of the well . . .
    a man—a Jew!
We Samaritans hate Jews.
They are enemy . . . foreign . . . different.
We keep away from them
and they from us.
But I am so thirsty.

He is watching me.

"Woman, give me water."

(How dare he!)
How dare he even speak to me,
let alone ask a favor!
Jews are not permitted
to speak to Samaritans,

especially a woman!
Doesn't he know the rules?!
He must be mad.
But he looks kindly
upon me.
(Oh, don't let me weep
because of kindness!)

I am just thirsty . . .
He does not know
I am a harlot
or he would stone me!
"Give me water."

Is he serious?
Does he not know
the law—the rules?

I am so thirsty . . .

"I will give you Living Water."
Ha!
What is he talking about?!
Mad . . . mad.
But he seems so gentle.
He is looking at me
as if he really cares!
No one has ever cared . . .

I am so thirsty.

What is this "Living Water"?

Something in me stirs.
It is a longing,
a hunger so deep
I feel the pain of it
in my very guts.

Living Water?

I am so thirsty . . .
Give it to me!
Give me this Living Water!
He talks to me,
tells me my own story,
piercing my heart with his knowledge
of who and what I am.

He knows me—
all of me—
all the hidden, nasty stuff!
But he doesn't strike me
or spit on me.
He looks tenderly
with compassion.
No one has ever looked upon me
with gentleness,
like a brother—
a real brother!
Suddenly I am
no longer alone.

This foreigner, this alien,
whom my people and culture
tell me to hate,
is offering me new life
and hope
as if I were his sister,
instead of a harlot,
a sex worker!

I feel so different!
I feel so clean!
I have a brother!
I am family!
I feel so beloved!
It must be the water . . .
the living Water!
I am no longer thirsty!!

So I run, oh, so fast,
to tell the world,
to tell the foreigners, the aliens,
the enemies, the hookers
that there is water,
Living Water!
And it is for me,
for you,
for all of us!

Come.
Come to the water.

Rachel Carson
(1907–1964)

"To stand at the edge of the sea, to feel the breath of a mist moving over a great salt marsh, to watch the flight of shore birds that have swept up and down the surf lines for untold millions of years, is to have knowledge of things that are as nearly eternal as any earthy life can be. These things were before ever man stood on the shore of the ocean and looked out upon it with wonder; they continue year in, year out, through the centuries and the ages, while kingdoms rise and fall."

(Under the Sea-Wind)

Rachel Louise Carson was born on a farm near Springdale, Pennsylvania. As a youngster, she was an avid reader and enjoyed exploring her family's sixty-five acres of land. At age eight, she wrote her first story, and she published her first work when she was eleven. Her stories often involved animals.

After graduating from high school in 1925, Rachel attended the Pennsylvania College for Women. She first studied English, but was drawn to science and chose biology as her major. Rachel earned her master's degree in zoology in 1932 and hoped to pur-

sue her doctorate, but family traumas brought an end to her academic dreams, and she temporarily left academia to return home to support her family. While caring for both her mother and her father (who died suddenly in 1935), Rachel took a teaching position. In order to alleviate an increasingly dire financial situation, she accepted a position with the U.S. Bureau of Fisheries, which allowed her to write a series of radio educational broadcasts entitled "Romance Under the Water." Her work won the approval of her superiors and she was awarded a full-time position. She became only the second woman to be hired as a professional by the Bureau of Fisheries.

Rachel worked tirelessly, analyzing and reporting on fish life and making the public aware of the beauty of marine life. Within a year, the *Atlantic Monthly* accepted her essay "The World of Waters," published as "Under the Sea," which took readers on a tour of the ocean floor. Her writing took wings, and her career hit a major turning point.

Rachel's personal life with all its commitments to family did not deter her from following her heart's call, and by 1945 she stumbled upon DDT—a pesticide only beginning to be understood for its ecological effects. Her research on synthetic pesticides and their dangers consumed her energies for the remainder of her life. The result of her exhaustive study resulted in the publication of *Silent Spring* (1962), a work that brought environmental concerns directly to the American public and eventually led to the creation of the Environmental Protection Agency.

Carson's work did not win widespread approval as her critics were aggressive and fierce in their disapproval of her thesis. They accused her of suggesting a complete elimination of pesticides, while she encouraged only a responsible and careful management of chemicals within the whole of the ecosystem. Her scientific credentials and her character were attacked, but her cause became known in a world needing her wisdom.

Weakened by the ravages of breast cancer that gradually metastasized, she died of a heart attack on April 14, 1964. Rachel Carson—pioneer, biologist, writer, ecologist—continues to be remembered and celebrated. In 1980, she was posthumously awarded the Presidential Medal of Freedom by Jimmy Carter. A seventeen-cent Great American series stamp was issued in her honor and the Rachel Carson Bridge in Pittsburgh stands tall in tribute to this woman who stood tall for life.

No one was watching,
No one was listening . . .
But you were, Rachel,
solitary listener.
You heard with delight
the song of the birds
and observed the movement
of insects beneath the soil.
Peering beneath rocks and stones,
you watched,
awed and fascinated,
at the leaping of the fish
the scuttling of the crabs,
and the life and movement
of a thousand different species
of crawling and burying things.

You felt connected, Rachel,
to all that lived
and moved around you—
on land, and in sea and air.
Living in wonder and amazement,
you loved and embraced it all.
Every creature that breathed
held kinship for you.
You were a wanderer
amongst nature—
your refuge and your home.

And you knew,
without any doubt—
in the tradition of
St. Francis, Hildegard,
Mechtild, Teilhard de Chardin,
Thomas Berry, and many more—
prophets and saints—
that the beauty of nature
all around us
was an essential part
of our spirituality
and a source of healing
for the human spirit.
The migration of the birds,
the life span of the monarchs,
the ebb and flow of the tides,
and the certainty of the seasons
were all gifts

to calm and sustain the soul.
You believed, Rachel,
that if we could focus
on the wonders of the universe
and become conscious
of our interconnectedness
with nature,
we would protect our environment
with a passion!

It was this love and conviction
that eventually led you,
through enormous pain and trauma,
to birth the environmental movement
we know today.
Bringing together science,
biology, poetry, and writing,
you shared your knowledge
and insights with the world.
Your book
The Sea All Around Us
propelled you
into the public arena,
changing forever
your life of withdrawal
and retreat.
Your preoccupation with
creeping, crawling
and flying things, Rachel,
now belonged to the world.

It was a friend
who first alerted you
to the terrible tragedy
being wrought upon the birds,
the insects, the trees,
and the earth you so loved.
Aerial spraying
of the deadly chemical DDT
to kill mosquitoes
also destroyed a myriad other
living things.
Poisoned leaves
fell to the ground
and were eaten by the worms
that, filled with toxins,
were then eaten by the birds.
Thousands died
in terrible pain.
No one was watching.
But you were, Rachel.
No one was listening.
But you were, Rachel,
and you were listening to
the silent spring
when no birds sang.

No one noticed, Rachel,
but you did—
when they sprayed the wetlands
to kill the sand fly

and also destroyed
millions of fish, insects,
plants, and crabs—
all part of the interconnected,
delicate web of life.
You anguished, Rachel!
And you knew
that you could not keep silent.
As Catherine of Siena
proclaimed before you,
"It is silence which kills the world."
And so you spoke aloud—
a million words and more.
You declared
that we are all related.
When we poison nature,
we poison ourselves!
You must have felt
a gut-wrenching sickness
in your soul, Rachel.
Impassioned and driven,
a brilliant scientist and writer,
you did your research,
uncovering with horror
the relentless use
of deadly pesticides
on the earth
spawned by a huge and powerful
chemical industry
spraying their poisons

everywhere—
on farmland, in fish ponds, parks,
and playgrounds.
And you, yourself, Rachel,
became sick.

Was your body responding
to the arrogance of men?
Was your cancer
a symptom of the sickness
and the dying—all around you—
of the creatures you so loved?
Was your connection so real,
that you would die too?

Against a growing onslaught
from the powerful chemical industry,
you fought back, Rachel,
for the birds, the worms, and
all crawling creeping things,
revealing to the public
the poisoning of the earth
and all its creatures.
The industry responded
with rage, fury, and derision.
You were "hysterical woman,"
"emotional,"
"deluded,"
"paranoid," and
"communist menace."

Still you continued to write,
exposing the evil
being wrought
by human ignorance and greed.

But in the solitude
of your cottage by the sea,
you wept, Rachel,
lonely prophet,
voice in the wilderness.
You wept and grieved alone
as you listened to
the soothing music of Beethoven—
another great soul,
in touch, like you,
with a deep spirit
that fed and sustained
your soul,
keeping you anchored
to your passion.
Though longing to withdraw and hide,
you would not.
For the sake of the birds,
the insects, the fish,
the earth, and the trees,
you continued
your lonely, prophetic journey,
driven by the music in your soul
and an inner conviction that
no amount

of hatred and vitriol
could dispel.
For four long years
you wrote,
spilling out your terrifying research
in a single book
that would change
the course of history.
You poured out your energy and spirit
for the earth and its creatures.
But you yourself were dying.
No one knew.
But you did, Rachel.
Though weak and exhausted in body,
your spirit never faltered
in your struggle to save
the song of the birds.

Your book *Silent Spring*
became a turning point for
our world, Rachel,
as legislation was passed
to save and protect
our environment.

But nothing could protect
and save you, Rachel.
Your body spent and weakened,
death came soon after your book
was given to the world—

the last gift of a great lover.

You left us with your tears and
the words:
"I have done what I could."
Indeed, Rachel.
Indeed.
You did more,
much more,
than you would ever know.

Blessed are you, Rachel,
brave prophet,
steward of the earth
and lover
of all creation,
blessed are you!

May we continue your journey,
treating the earth
and all living creatures
as our sisters and brothers.

May we too,
as we listen to the song of the birds,
be able to declare:
"We are doing everything we can."

Sister Dorothy Stang
(1931–2005)

Dorothy Stang, SNDdeN, was born in Dayton, Ohio, and attended Julian High School. She left school responding to a call to religious life and joined the convent of the Sisters of Notre Dame de Namur in Cincinnati. The order is a strong proponent of liberation theology, focusing on the care of the poor, particularly of women and children in far removed, seemingly helpless locations.

Dorothy responded to her heart's call and set off to Brazil in the 1960s. The region she traversed held large tracts of rainforests and was fraught with many dangers. The threats came not from the wildness of the land, but from logging firms and ranchers who illegally exploited it. Her work with human rights activists to protect the land rights of the small farmer made her a target of big business. For thirty years Dorothy labored in Anapu, a town on the edge of the Amazon rainforest, organizing efforts to protect the environment from plunder. The locals affectionately called her "Dora" and "the Angel of Trans-Amazonian," while those who plotted to end her life considered her a terrorist

who gave guns to the peasant farmers to protect their families and their land.

Dorothy's last moments were spent with two peasants who accompanied her on the road (much like the scene on the road to Emmaus) to the Boa Esperança Settlement. This area rightfully belonged to the peasants but it was sought after by the loggers in the name of economic growth. They came for her here, on the road. They shot her six times in the head, in the throat, in the body, at close range and left her in the mud to die. Her Bible, from which she had been reading to the assassins fell to the ground: "Blessed are the poor in spirit for theirs is the Kingdom of God" (Mt 5:3).

Six bullets echoed
through the forest
that awful day.
They felled
the petite, elderly nun
clasping her Bible,
and silenced her gentle voice
as she read the Beatitudes
to her killers:
"Blessed are the peace-makers . . ."

The shots turned her white hair
Red, like the forest soil
she loved so much,
and her blood fed

and moistened the earth.
Sister Dorothy—
Champion of the poor,
Voice of the indigenous,
Lover of the little ones,
Disciple of Jesus.
Dorothy, the little nun,
so beloved,
was dead
and only the forest
she loved and protected
knew it,
and
in stunned silence,
witnessed the violence
of it all.

For forty years
Dorothy loved and served
the peasants of Brazil
as they struggled
to protect and farm their land
in the shadow
of the mighty Amazon.
Her voice,
for such a small and aging body,
rang strong and clear
in defense of the poor
as loggers and corporations—
accountable to none—

sought to steal the people's land
and fell the timber
for marketing and profit.

Dorothy,
the little nun,
was a problem.
She was in the way,
as she stood
like a great protective mother
shielding her family,
the people and the trees
of the Amazon,
from corporate power and greed.
She knew of the threats.
She could have fled
to the safety of Ohio
and the comfort
of her own people
back in the States.

But Dorothy was a lover
who had been seized
by a passionate God
to follow a life
of commitment and service
in a foreign land.
This God, this love,
this purpose,
was to Dorothy

bigger than all fear
and all intimidation.

So she stayed
in spite of the threats,
loyal to a far higher power
than global, corporate giant.

This, indeed,
is what greatness is all about.
This, indeed,
is what holiness is all about—
the faithful and dogged pursuit of
justice and goodness,
no matter what the sacrifice.
No matter what the cost.

You gave your life, Dorothy,
for love,
for values and principles
that honor human dignity
and the integrity
of all creation.

You gave your life
for the mighty yet vulnerable trees
that provide all livings things
with oxygen.
You gave your life, Dorothy,
for all of us

who could never dare
to walk your path
but long for the witness
and inspiration
of your courage and selflessness
in a world of fear and greed.

We honor you,
small, magnificent woman!
And we pray that your witness
will give us light
to see more clearly
what we must do
to follow your path
in our own ways
wherever we live and work.

May your martyrdom, Dorothy,
give us courage
to stand upright,
calling for justice and
the protection of the earth.
We will not die for justice,
as you did,
but let us deeply live for it.
And may we dare
to cry aloud, like you,
small, passionate woman,
before the threats,
the bombs and the bullets

and the false power of greed and evil,
declaring in the face
of all violence:
"Blessed are the peace-makers . . ."

And blessed are you,
Dorothy, saint of the Amazon.

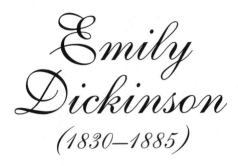

Emily Dickinson
(1830–1885)

Emily Dickinson was born in Amherst, Massachusetts, on December 10, 1830, to a highly respected family within the local community. Her home was frequently visited by distinguished visitors, most notable among them Ralph Waldo Emerson.

Emily, from an early age, was a bright student capturing her classmates' attention with her ability to create rhyming stories.

She grew into a beautiful young lady with deep dark eyes and a soft voice. A quick wit and a charming sense of humor were attractive qualities of this simply dressed, unadorned woman who often was uncomfortable in social settings or in the company of others.

Her father exerted a strong influence over the upbringing of his children, insisting that they be raised in the most respectable and proper way. Emily often struggled with her desire to be "the best little girl," because she was more comfortable being independent. Her independence was most evident in her religious beliefs (often surfacing in her poetry). She did not adhere to the teachings of Calvin—a dominant religious belief system in nineteenth-century New England that viewed "men" as sinful and most humans

doomed to hell. Pressures were put on Emily at school to join the "saved," but she chose her own path, remaining true to her "inner stirrings" and aloof from orthodox religion. Much of this sentiment muses through her poetry as she wrote of "being shut out of heaven." Her most profound "religious" experiences came from her love of creation's beauty within nature. The depth of her inner experiences fills her poetry with passion.

Emily studied at Mount Holyoke Female Seminary in South Hadley, Massachusetts. Intrigued by a wide range of subjects, she delved into Latin and English literature. She was an artist and musician, but her studies were interrupted when she took ill, and her father removed her from school and brought her home.

It is said that at the age of 20 she lived a life of seclusion in her family's dwelling. This by no means closed her mind to the words that flowed from the deeper recesses that dwelt within her.

Benjamin Newton, a young law student introduced to her by her brother, recognized Emily's gift for poetry and encouraged her to write. She read the works of other poets, especially Emerson, and this pushed her to conquer her own doubts and led her to trust her own convictions, opening her to new spiritual ideas beyond Calvinism.

Political concerns (strong traditions with her family) and the war were not embraced by Emily. However, when many of her closest friends died during the Civil War, a strong chord was struck, and fear and death preoccupied her and dominated the most productive years of her writing. In addition to some 1,800 known poems, she was a prolific letter writer. Her life of seclusion and her poor health did not dampen her profound joy. She was a mystic and able to see beyond the strains of the world. Emily died at the early age of 55.

Emily—
A little bit of God
got lost on earth and
ever seeking
your way home!
Emily—
Mystic in the closet,
whispering love poems
in the darkness.
Emily—
deep contemplative,
devoid of cloister or choir
except for
the song of the birds.

Your adult life was spent
in solitude—
not monastic cell or
behind convent walls—
but in your bedroom at home,
overlooking the world
with all its bustle and action
beneath your open window.
But your door
was always closed,
allowing you to enter
the soul's domain within
where you slept, lived,

and loved the shadows
of your sacred space.

"The soul selects her own society,"
you wrote,
"then shuts the door."

Indeed you did.
For 30 years you sat
pondering by your bedroom window,
seeking and cherishing
"eternity's disclosure,"
glimpsing and capturing
the heaven
you then shared with us all
on scraps of paper—
spiritual masterpieces—
scrawled on the backs of recipes
and grocery lists
then tied together with string.

You were in love, Emily.
All of your silent, reclusive life
you were in love with
the hidden, the ethereal,
the deeps of the soul.
You engaged the heavy questions
of life and death and suffering.
Living in mystery
you embraced enigma,

questioning and challenging
the God you did not understand,
but honored:

"I know He exists,
somewhere—in the Silence—
He has hid His rare life
from our gross eyes."

Ah, Emily, you sensed the divine,
not in holy books or churches,
but in the wonder of nature
that displayed its shapes
and colors and songs,
like an ever-changing painting
outside your window.
Your words were mystic prayer:
"Some keep the Sabbath going to church—
I keep it staying at home—
With a bobolink [songbird] for a chorister
And an orchard for a dome.

Some keep the Sabbath in surplice—
I just wear my wings—
And instead of tolling the bell for church,
Our little sexton [songbird] sings.

God preaches, a noted Clergyman—
And the sermon is never long,
So, instead of getting to heaven, at last—
I'm going all along."

Indeed, Emily—
"Dwelling in possibility,"
you were going all along!

As your journey deepened
you wore only white,
to symbolize, I think,
the purity of divine love
and your intense quest for truth.
Shunning all dogma and creed,
you believed in a more immediate God
manifest in trees, flowers, birds,
and the great canopy of the sky.
God was mystery, yet a Presence,
Which captured you:

"I dwell in Possibility—
A fairer House than Prose—
More numerous of Windows—
Superior—for Doors—

Of Chambers as the Cedars—
Impregnable of Eye—
And for the Everlasting Roof
The Gambrels of the Sky—

Of Visitors—the fairest—
For Occupation—This—
The spreading wide of narrow Hands—
To gather Paradise—"
You left us

that glimpse of Paradise, Emily—
1,800 soul poems—
your "Letter to the world,"
born in silence
and delivered in death,
discovered only after you yourself
had left us,
returned from exile and
free, at last,
to be dissolved into eternity.

No need now
To close the door.

We thank you, Emily,
Mystic in the closet,
for allowing us
a glimpse of your longings
and a fleeting glance
at your persistent
quest for God.

May we, too,
close the door
to listen in the silence of our souls,
pondering long and deeply
the Mystery that moves
in us all.

"Where Thou art—that is home."

Julian of Norwich
(1342–ca. 1416)

J ulian was born in England during the days of the plague known as the Black Death. We know little of her—not even her real name—as she was named Julian only after the Church where she lived as an anchorite for most of her adult life.

The Black Death pervaded her era as did poverty, unemployment, wars with France, religious persecution, high taxation, political unrest, and bad harvests. In spite of all this, Julian maintained a joyful and deep faith in the presence of Christ, which began with a near-death experience when she was thirty-three during which she received the Last Rites. At the point of death she had a vision of the crucified Christ, and she experienced instant healing. The vision was followed by sixteen others—all within two days. These visions changed and dominated the rest of her life.

Desiring to be more closely united with God, Julian chose a life of contemplation and prayer as an anchoress living a solitary life—not removed from the world, but anchored in it. She lived in a small cell attached to St. Julian's church in Norwich.

Her cell had a window looking into the church so she was able to participate in the Mass and receive the Sacraments. A second window looked out onto the street enabling passers by to seek Julian's counsel and advice.

Julian's book *Revelations of Divine Love* is her gift to the world and the result of years spent contemplating her visions. It conveys her passion for Jesus as loving and joyful Savior and describes Jesus as intimately close to us as our clothing. Julian's visions focus on the Passion of Christ—but in spite of His sufferings and the reality of sin, she experienced Jesus as over-joyed with love for humanity and was assured: "All will be well, and all will be well . . ."—words of great comfort for our contemporary world.

They called you Julian.
But you weren't Julian.
That was only the name
of the small church
where you lived
for most of your life
in a little stone room
attached to the wall of
St. Julian in the medieval city of
Norwich in England.

What drove you, Julian,
to spend your life in a stone cell
in the inner city?

Ah, it was love,
pure, focused, passionate love
that seized and impelled you
to give your life
to the Christ who revealed to you
His Passion
for all humanity.

You fell in love, Julian,
so deeply, so intensely,
that you could do no other
than lock yourself
in a tiny space
to be consumed
by love
and to listen—deeply.

But all around
your silent cell, Julian,
the world bustled
and cried aloud
in frenzied activity.
People bartered their wares,
traded their goods,
and begged for alms.
The noise and clamor of the city
never ceased;
the stink of open sewers
and the smell
of burning flesh (unmistakable)

from the victims of the
Papal Inquisition,
drifted past your dwelling
and through
your open window.
And every night, Julian,
the dead were collected,
on carts and
carried from nearby hovels
as the Black Death,
stalking the city relentlessly,
claimed its daily victims.

War raged
between France and England,
and in the countryside
battles between feudal lords
and starving peasants
continued relentlessly.
And there you were, Julian,
Dame of Norwich,
on your knees
in the heart of it all,
consumed by love
in the midst of hatred,
war,
and downright evil.

So the stricken people
came to you, Julian,

weeping, grieving, lost:
"Why are we suffering, Dame Julian?
Help us!
Speak to us!"
You were their only anchor
in a swirling sea
of violence and pain.
"Julian, Julian—
What have you to say?
Where is God?
Why are we dying?
Speak to us, Dame of Norwich!"
And, rising from the love
in which you were enclosed
and anchored,
came your response,
spoken with deep conviction,
the words that still resonate
with us today—centuries on:

"All will be well.
And all will be well.
And all manner of things
will be well."

No quick fix.
No fast, instant solution.
No band-aids.
No false gratification.

Just a deep, deep conviction
born of prayer, faith,
and the words of Christ
rising in your consciousness that,
right in the midst
of human chaos, evil, and darkness—
God, eternal Lover,
dwells,
rooted in our humanity,
loving us,
holding us
through all of it.
God is with us.
God is with us—
in all the hell—
God is with us.

This, Julian,
was your message
that still
speaks to us today.

Bemused and wondering
you saw a vision:
See, here,
in the palm of my hand,
a tiny hazelnut . . .
What can it mean?
Then the words of God

came breaking into
the consciousness
of Julian, the lover:

It is all,
all that is made
in the palm
of God's hand.
Indeed. Indeed.
Julian, Dame of Norwich!
It was given to you
to share with us all
that God holds us
in the palm of God's hand
and will never,
can never,
let us go.

And all will be well.
And all will be well.
And all manner of things
will be well.

Be comforted,
Be comforted, my people,
says your God.

Blessed Mother Teresa
(1910–1997)

"Holiness is not the luxury of the few, but a simple duty for you and me." Such are the words spoken often by the woman diminutive in stature but strongly independent in spirit.

Gonxha (Agnes) Bojaxhir was born on August 27, 1910, in Skooje, Yugoslavia, one of five children (three of whom survived). Her father, Nikola, was a successful building contractor and merchant who provided his family with comforts beyond those afforded to peasants. Their lifestyle was described by her brother Lazar as "lacking for nothing." Her mother Dronda was devoted to her husband and children and provided for their daily needs—cooking, cleaning, and mending. Dronda's religious practices, performed lovingly but without undue attention ("When you do good, do it quietly, as if you were throwing a stone into the sea") deeply influenced young Agnes who often accompanied her mother on journeys of mercy, and no doubt, planted the seed for the young girl's life of giving her "all." The close-knit family enjoyed time together for only a brief time as her father died suddenly when Agnes was eight, and her brother

Lazar joined the army and then emigrated to Italy. After Agnes left for India in 1928, she never again saw her sister Aga or her mother.

A religious vocation began to stir in Agnes' heart at the age of twelve and came to fruition when she entered the Sisters of Loreto of Dublin (missionaries and teachers) at eighteen. Agnes spent much time and energy learning to speak English—working hard—observing life around her and adapting to the disciplines of convent life. In 1931, she professed vows and took the name Sister Teresa in honor of both Teresa of Avila and Thérèse of Lisieux. Her years with the Sisters of Loreto were spent teaching wealthy young women but despite her dedication to her ministry her sights were set elsewhere.

In 1946, she headed for a retreat in Darjeeling and the overwhelming poverty she witnessed tugged at her heartstrings. Here again she was "called" to teach and to serve as the school's principal. When she shared this news with her mother, she was sternly reminded to "not forget that you went to India for the sake of the poor."

In 1948, with permission from Pope Pius XII, Teresa left the Sisters of Loreto, received the blessing of the Archbishop of Calcutta, and began her sacred journey into the city slums.

To prepare for her new life, Teresa went to Patna to study nursing. Life in Calcutta, upon her return, was difficult and challenging, but she made immediate in-roads by creatively teaching hygiene to children using whatever "tools" she could find. In no time word of her outreach spread and crowds reached out to her for care and compassion. Within a year, she was joined by other young women who came to offer their services. They became the foundation of the new order of the Missionaries of Charity, formally approved on October 7, 1950.

For more than fifty years the Missionaries of Charity, with Mother Teresa at the helm, served those most in need. Homes for the dying, treatment centers for alcoholics, hospitals for those with leprosy, centers for children—always the children—to be taught and cared for, outreach to the aged and the street people— all were possible as food, clothing, money, medical supplies, and other services were offered to the sisters from all over the world. Whatever the need—from whomever it came, Mother Teresa responded in LOVE. She saw herself as "God's pencil—a tiny bit of pencil with which He writes what He likes."

Never seeking personal accolades, but always with her gaze upon the God she so loved and upon the poor to whom she ministered, the world continues to be in awe of "all" that this little woman was able to accomplish and showered her with numerous honors, among them the 1979 Nobel Peace Prize and the 2010 U.S. Stamp issued in her name.

Mother Teresa died on September 5, 1997.

On October 19, 2003, six years after her death, Pope John Paul II beatified Mother Teresa, calling her "one of the greatest missionaries of the twentieth century."

Amazing
that such a small, fragile woman
could shake an apathetic world
with the grace of God,
as you did, Teresa,
woman in love with Jesus.

You shook the world
because you were in love—
a deep and all-consuming love
that left us all
a little blinded.
It is rare
that we see such light
in our dark and frightened world.
But you shone, little woman,
and all of us,
from plumber to president,
saw it.

"Come, be My light"
were the words
that seized your soul
and thrust you into heaven,
and then to hell.
From that time on,
impelled by your soul's light
to live in darkness,
loving the destitute,
you never wavered
little woman of God.
Propelled by love,
you brought it
into dark and dirty places
like a great Resurrection
shining in the tombs
of the dying.

So convinced and consumed were you,
that you pestered and begged
the hierarchy of the Church
to approve and bless your call.
With Jesus you waited
four years for approval
to found your dream—
the Missionaries of Charity.
And then, oh, then,
how this plant
burst into blossom
in the poorest corners
of the globe!
Like the mustard seed
that grows into
a mighty tree,
your work of love
increased and spread,
thrusting its healing branches
all over our broken world.
Ah, passionate lover of Jesus!
You took His light
into the last moments
of the dying
so that they could see and know
that in their very misery
they were held in love,
seeing in your eyes
the first light of the heaven
that awaited them.

The great ones of the world
applauded and honored you,
little woman of God,
amazed at your shining light
and peacefulness.
In the midst of the horror
surrounding you—
still you were radiant.
They did not know
that your light
shielded and hid
your own terrible
inner darkness.
For, in all the many years
of your serving and loving,
you had lost
the early delight
of knowing and feeling
the presence of Christ.

The honeymoon was dead.
Long dead.
It was as if, perhaps,
the poverty and desolation
of those you served
now lived within you
as well
as all around you.

But you kept on going,

little lover of Jesus,
without the love.
You followed the call
you could no longer hear,
insanely faithful
to the Lover who left you
in darkness.
Love unrequited.
(But is that not what Jesus did?
He poured his love
upon the earth and all he met
and ended up
in death and darkness—
love unrequited.)

The hunger for love
ravaged your fragile self,
little woman of God.
But so intense
was your faithfulness
that you offered
your very emptiness to the Christ
by whom you felt abandoned.
Ah, no one could imagine
your secret pain and loneliness
as you were showered
with applause and honor.
No one either
could imagine
the depth of your enduring love

which shone, never faltering,
until your own light
was extinguished.
And now,
Mother Teresa, woman of God,
now that you are gone,
we are left aghast
at the power of true love
which you personified;
we are left to ponder
and to pray,
that we might come
to love one another—
even a little bit—
just a little bit more—
because now, in you,
we are reminded yet again,
that love is possible
and that love transforms all things:
"By their fruits, you shall know them."
Indeed, we know you . . .

Blessed are you, Mother Teresa,
little woman. Great lover.

"Come be My light".

Lucy Wisdom
(1956–2009)

"Swinging from the trees is really what it is cracked up to be. . . ."

Lucy Wisdom, the oldest of four children and the only girl born to parents who were both doctors in London, always seemed to follow the road less traveled. At 16, with her parents' blessing, Lucy set off to work on a kibbutz in Israel, launching into a life of adventure, travel ... and care.

Lucy studied at Bristol University reading geology and archaeology. After graduation she set off to India, Australia, New Zealand, and Indonesia taking on small jobs to help pay for the next step in countless journeys. In London, Lucy trained in circus skills. Much to her parents' bewilderment, she and her brothers engaged in a triple act known as the Wisdom Brothers. The act combined acrobatics, juggling, and trapeze ... and Lucy's escapology performance. Lucy went on to work with her other brother as a tour manager assisting the band "Specimen."

Always lured to newness and adventure, she crewed a yacht to Barbados in 1982, staying only to create an Archeological Society. (This adventure continued for ten additional years after she left.)

Lucy joined a group of performance artists/sculptors known as the Mutoid Waste Co. This act created uncanny events involving mutated materials—cars, cranes, and planes—as backdrops while swinging acrobatically in bizarre, outlandish costumes while percussionists played.

Life as Lucy knew it came to a crashing halt when she was diagnosed with breast cancer in 1994. Following surgery, she went to Sumatra voluntarily to help the Orangutan Rehabilitation Centre at Bohorok. Cancer changed her life and she calmly responded, "Changing what you are doing is the holistic approach. Cancer suggests you are doing something that is not in line with your life." She spent five years swinging through towering trees helping young orangutans learn skills they did not have an opportunity to develop from their parents.

The more time she spent with the apes, the more she sensed that saving them did not halt their imminent extinction. She set up the Sumatran Orangutan Society (SOS) to protect the apes' habitat, which was being lost to logging, burning, and palm oil plantations. She wasted neither time nor energy in her conservation work and met with primatologists and animal rights activists when she traveled to the International Great Ape Conference in Borneo. She realized how significant the orangutans were to the rainforest ecosystem and labored tirelessly to preserve the species.

Lucy's achievements were not left unrewarded personally and professionally. SOS evoked a collaborate policy with Sumatran programs financing conservation classes, road shows, planting schemes, and eco-treks. Lucy was awarded Hero of the Month by Marie Claire Magazine and Ethical Businesswoman in 2009.

Upon her death in December 2009, her life's voice could be heard in the forests that she so loved and in the orangutans whom she sought to protect.

~

Cancer.
You knew your time
was running out, Lucy.
Little by little
the cancerous cells
were spreading their destruction—
devastating your once
vital, healthy body.
But not before
you became aware
of another dying—
that of the Sumatra orangutans
at the other end of the world
from your English home.
It was your very cancer
that impelled you
to save the dying
of another species.
Filled with a passion for life,
the orangutans became
your reason for living.
You could not save yourself
but you could save
something else.

The orangutans—
intelligent, affectionate
acrobats of the trees.

were natural performers—
swinging from the high
outstretched branches—
created by a God who delights
in diversity and play.
Until the forest home of
these wild yet playful apes
was increasingly threatened
and destroyed by loggers
with chain saws,
bulldozers and burning.
The orangutans
were killed, captured for sale,
or died of devastation.

You knew about dying, Lucy.
It was before you constantly
in your own wasting body,
and you saw it again
in the wasting trees,
the dwindling habitat,
and the loss of the home
of the orangutans.
But you knew about life too, Lucy.
For you had trained
as an acrobat and juggler,
leaping from trapeze to trapeze
in huge circus domes,
with vitality and ease,
just like the orangutans.

With the loss of their habitat
many of the young
became orphaned,
losing not only their home
but also the parents and elders
who had taught them
how to climb and swing
in their forest home.

Creative, imaginative, and
lusting for life,
you, Lucy, became
their surrogate
mother and teacher.
For five years you shared
their lives,
teaching the orphaned young
how to climb the vines and
swing through the trees—
skills vital for survival.

You stood over and against
the powers of greed and evil—
one little woman—
a David against Goliath—
with a passion and a fire
bright and brilliant.
You leapt, Lucy,
into the cause of conservation,
education, fundraising,

habitat protection, eco-treks and
tree planting
with a vigor that defied
your own wasting body.
One little woman—
determined to save
those she could,
though not herself.
You knew that time
was running out for you—
and the orangutans—
but, to the very end,
you gave every ounce of
the life left in you
to save the forest apes.

You died too soon, Lucy,
lover of creation and protector
of its leaping creatures.
But you left behind
a legacy of love and action
to remind us
that all living things
are precious,
and all creation—
smooth or furred—
reflects divinity.
"It's about what you believe,"
you declared.
Indeed it is, Lucy.

It is all about what we believe.
May we too, Lucy,
woman of the forest,
believe enough
to protect and save
the threatened and the dying.
May we, too, honor and respect
the creatures of the earth
and the habitat—rightfully theirs.

Blessed and holy are you, Lucy,
sister of the orangutans.

Pema Chödrön
(1936–)

"Life has taught me the wisdom of moving toward what scares me...."

Deirdre Blomfield-Brown, known to the world as Pema Chödrön, was born in New York City. Her family, including an older brother and sister, moved to New Jersey when Deirdre was a young child. She was raised Catholic and attributes the development of her spiritual journey to her school experiences, most notably Miss Porter's School in Farmington, Connecticut, and Sarah Lawrence College in Bronxville, New York. During this time of spiritual awakening, Deirdre found herself engaged in a deeper intellectual quest. Her time at Sarah Lawrence was short-lived; in 1957, at the age of 21, she left home and collegiate life to marry.

Her daughter, Arlyn, was born a year after she married, followed three years later by her son, Edward. Deirdre moved to Berkeley, California, in 1961 where she pursued studies at UC Berkeley earning a BA in English literature and an MA in elementary education. She worked as an elementary school teacher for many years in California and New Mexico. After her first marriage ended, she remarried and relocated to Taos, New Mexico, with her husband and children. When her second husband admitted to having an affair, and asked for a divorce, she later reflected: "There was no time, no thoughts, there was nothing—just the light and a profound, limitless stillness. Then I regrouped and picked up a stone and threw it at him." Life, for Deirdre, had hit a turning point.

After her second marriage ended, Deirdre embarked on a search for answers. She explored various spiritual traditions but none seemed to touch her "soul" until she met and began to study with Lama Chime Rinpoche in the French Alps. Soon she was introduced to Chogyam Trungpa Rinpoche with whom she made a deep connection and with whom she worked from 1974 until his death in 1987. She explored what Trungpa, her root guru, taught and practiced the tenets of the Buddhist way with deep determination and with profound joy.

In 1981, Pema Chödrön (her Buddhist name meaning "Lotus Dharma Torch") received the full bhikshuni ordination in the Chinese lineage of Buddhism in Hong Kong—the only English-speaking and Western person to be admitted to the rite. Four years later (1985) Chogyam Trungpa urged Pema to establish Gampo Abbey in Nova Scotia—the first Tibetan Buddhist monastery in North America for Western men and women. She did so and became the director of the abbey and of its retreat center in 1986. Here she published the first two of the many books she has since written. Since 1990, she has established residency at the abbey sharing her ideas, guiding new monks and nuns, and teaching courses.

Years of teaching, travel, talks, retreat work, media events of all sorts have taken their toll on Pema's health. Chronic fatigue-immune dysfunction syndrome as well as environmental illness forced her to undertake a long-term course of healing. "It required me to simplify my life, a very sane thing to do."

Aside from the countless books she authors and the retreats she offers around the world, this Catholic American-born woman, ordained Buddhist nun, touches countless numbers of persons because of who she is. Pema inspires all those who yearn for what cries deep within them. She shares her wisdom and teachings and offers pathways to get "unhooked" from the emotions of fear, anger, and low-self esteem that hold persons back from themselves.

You began
as Deirdre Bloomfield-Brown,
elementary teacher from New York,
and you ended up
as Pema Chödrön,
the first American Buddhist nun
and one of the greatest
spiritual teachers of our time.

We stand in awe
of such a journey—
spanning the globe
and stretching
an ordinary wife and mother
into one of those rare lights
shining for us all.
Wisdom figure,
great teacher,
spiritual warrior.

How does one hurtle from
the ordinary and mundane
into those kinds of
sacred spaces?

For you, Deirdre,
it was pain—
the emotional stress
of two broken marriages
that left you
all broken up,
in deep depression,
and desperate to flee
the anguish,
like most of us.
We have all been there.
Many still are.
What are we to do with
our anger, pain, and emotions?
What are we to do
about the violence of our world
and the fear
in our own hearts?

That is why
you became a seeker, Deirdre,
looking for answers,
healing, and relief
from human suffering.
Until you met a wisdom figure—
a Tibetan Buddhist teacher

who became your friend and guide.
You found a new path,
and you followed it faithfully.

You learnt to breathe deeply,
mindfully—
breathing in awareness
and breathing out the pain
in steady, gentle consciousness—
the root practice of
meditation.

You befriended the pain
and stayed with it,
embracing and thus transforming,
through vulnerability and acceptance,
the anguish of your broken life.

Over the years,
and through long,
persistent practice,
you continued to face and accept,
with compassion and gentleness,
all that you were,
just as you were.
This is the process whereby
the ironclad soul
softens and gentles
into loving awareness.
With no cause now
to fight, resist, or rage,

you became calm and still,
freed from the power
of the demons that
possess us all.

You became
contemplative woman and
spiritual warrior,
breathing love and gentleness
upon our hurting world.
There was no magic.

No big miracle—
just a deep surrender
to reality
and a receptive openness
to being utterly present
to the very moment.
It is the moment
that is the teacher,
and that revealed to you, Pema,
the deep, profound joy
of your Oneness with all being—
the secret inheritance,
claimed by few
but belonging to all.

"Deirdre" became
Pema Chödrön—
"Lamp of the truth."

A new name
for a new and deeper life
in which there is no goal,
no target, no agenda,
no plan, no future—
but only the Journey of Awareness
and acceptance
that we walk—now,
totally present,
in compassion for oneself
and all for all beings.

And so you rose, Pema,
spiritual warrior,
 from your past cocoon
of negativity and stress,
to befriend your own
inner being
and thus become
teacher for us all,
insisting on the reality
of the basic grace and goodness
lodged deep within each
of our defensive, frightened selves,
waiting only
to be recognized, received, and embraced.
You teach
through your own struggle
and fearless journeying,
that we are

already blessed—tho' broken,
and our souls are big enough
to embrace
all that we are
and all that is
with peace and equanimity.
You challenge us, Pema,
to confront, tame, and befriend
our inner violence and fears
that we might soften into
our essential
contemplative selves
and become the transformed beings
we are all called to be.
Oh, for the sake of our planet
and for the sake
of our young,
may we, Pema,
spiritual warrior,
wise woman, guide, and teacher,
follow your path
into the deeper, truer life
that awaits all of us.

Mechtild of Magdeburg

(ca. 1207/8–ca. 1282/94)

Mechtild of Magdeburg was born into a family of nobility and grew up in a castle surrounded by courtly culture. At the age of twelve she experienced the first of many mystical visions. Around the age of twenty she joined the Beguines, choosing a selfless "descent" from the castle that had afforded her many luxuries and renouncing it in order to dwell in the city amongst the poor.

Mechtild lived and worked as a Beguine for some forty years. Beguines were independent lay women in thirteenth-century Europe who followed a lifestyle of poverty and good works, living in community and presenting the laity with a new and radical way of living out the Christian life.

The Crusades left many women and children without husbands or support, resulting in much poverty, and the Beguines responded to the needs of the time with creative ministry. Their primary concern was for the poor—particularly women and children. The Beguine lifestyle, unsupported by relatives or husbands,

was a threat to institutionalized religion and drew the displeasure of the clergy.

Mechtild is best known for her book *The Flowing Light of the Godhead*, which describes her love for God in terms of bridal mysticism. Her writings are passionate and poetic. But bitterly critiquing church corruption and abuse, she was forced to write "on the run" and was condemned by the Pope as a "loose woman."

Demoralized, persecuted, and suffering from loneliness, Mechtild eventually withdrew from her busy and harassed life and secluded herself in the convent of Helfta around 1270. It became one of the most important centers of female mysticism in the Middle Ages. Mechtild stands as one of the greatest and bravest female German mystics.

Ah, Mechtild of Magdeburg,
you fell in love with God
as a child
and ran with the joy of it!
All the days of your life
your love affair drove you
into a secular wilderness,
leaving family and security
to pursue the elusive ecstasy
of your burning love
for God.
But your wilderness
was fraught with danger
as your dance of love

played out
in the midst of church corruption,
abuse, and an institution
wedded to clerical power.
In the face of blatant sin and evil,
you poured out your pain
and anger
daring to declare
the judgment of God
on the men of God.

But who were you, Mechtild—
a lay woman
with not a vestige of authority
or a shred of status—
in an all-male institution!

How dared you speak aloud,
with such power and conviction,
in the midst
of the dreaded Inquisition
which sought out and condemned
any infraction of its
severe religious code?
Only the madness of love,
deeply felt and known,
would risk such folly.
It was a dangerous time,
and you, Mechtild,
were a dangerous woman,

condemned seventeen times
by the Pope as
"a loose woman"!
"Loose" because
you were free, Mechtild!
Your experience of God
freed you to be yourself,
secure in the knowledge that
"love is all,"
and that, before it,
we must all be free from fear.

So immersed in God were you
that you likened
the soul in God
to a bird in the sky,
a fish in the water.

The bird cannot fly
without air,
the fish cannot live
without water,
and you knew, Mechtild,
that you could not live
without God
who comes to us
as "dew on the flowers."
God, you wrote,
"is sick with love" for us—
"burning with desire"!

It was that passion, Mechtild,
that drove you
to speak and write
of the "hot love" for God
that burned within you
like a flame
that could not be quenched
by any human fear.
It is no wonder, Mechtild,
that the dried-up men
of the Inquisition feared
 your flowing feminine passion!
"God," you declared,
"is infinite freedom,"
who calls us into a deep,
personal relationship
that no one and no thing
can destroy or take away.
"See, there within the flesh,
like a bright wick englazed,
the soul that God's finger lit
to give her liberty."
A dangerous message indeed
for a church bound
by "the letter of the law"!
And so, you wrote
"on the run," Mechtild,
a holy fugitive
moving from place to place,
writing your poems,

and singing your songs of love.
Prolific with metaphors—
God, you understood, was like
a Great Mother
who bends down to lift her child
from the ground to Her bosom.
God was like
a Great Physician
who brings medicine and ointment
to heal the bruises
of His people.
Ah, God is our Playmate
who longs
to lead the child in us!

Yet for all your ecstasy and delight,
you also knew, Mechtild,
of the withdrawal of joy,
the descent into hell,
the darkness of abandonment,
and the absence of God—
as real as the presence of God:

"My Beloved has fled
while I was sleeping . . ."

We all know about the absences.
They are part of the journey
and part of the loving
that also must be received

and welcomed
just as mountains give way
to valleys.
It is all to be embraced . . .
For God,
Mechtild knew,
is like a Great Magnet,
and we are a needle.
Ultimately, kicking, screaming,
sinning, falling,
crying, loving,
God will bring us home.

May your message,
your poetry,
and your songs of love
help bring us home, too, Mechtild.
May God come to our souls
like the dew on the flowers
and may we, too,
hear God's voice
in the song of the birds.

Blessed are you, Mechtild,
lover, mystic, poet, and
Woman of courage.

Annie Dodge Wauneka
(1910–1997)

"I have been aware of the problems of my tribe (Navajo) and have wanted to help make our people aware of them."

Annie Dodge Wauneka, tribal leader of the Navajo nation and public health activist, was born in 1910 to Henry Chee Dodge, the last Chief of the Navajos, and his wife Kee'hanabob. She was raised by her father, who taught her effective skills of leadership.

Annie studied the ways of the Navajos and was deeply influenced by the history and culture of her people.

When Annie was eight years old, the government school she attended on the reservation in Fort Defiance, Arizona, was stricken with an influenza epidemic that took the lives of many of her classmates and left Annie, who escaped with only a mild case, to assist an overworked nurse in caring for those who were too ill to tend to their most basic needs. This tragic event shaped the rest of her life.

Although she left school in eleventh grade, her most prominent

teacher was her father whose ideas and stories stirred her heart. He taught her to "respect" others—most especially her elders.

After her marriage to George Wauneka, she lived in various places and traveled with her father to observe the poverty and disease that affected the Navajos. Drawn to that which plagued her people, she earned a degree in public health in hopes that she might influence the standards of health and sanitation. She eventually sought elected office and was the second woman to gain a seat on the Tribal Council (1951).

"If I fail, I will just go and do more."

Annie Dodge Wauneka—listener, learner, teacher, doer—did whatever she could to improve the quality of life for her people. She led the fight to eliminate tuberculosis and alcohol abuse, to improve sanitary conditions, and to provide better care for pregnant women and newborns. She served as a spokesperson to give the Indian people a voice in the location of their schools and found ways to influence legislation to help finance the building of new and different homes for the Navajos. She worked tirelessly to encourage her people to accept modern medical practices and to visit the hospital when necessary. She wrote a dictionary in the Navajo language to explain modern medical techniques and conducted a weekly radio broadcast for two years in her tribe's language to explain to her people how to take advantage of medical practices that would improve their lives. Her efforts did not go unnoticed, and she was invited to serve on the advisory boards of the U.S. Surgeon General and the U.S. Public Health Service. Her membership on the board enabled the U.S. Public Health Service and the Navajo medicine men to work together.

Those in the presence of this stately, striking tall woman whose traditional Navajo garb included her colorful shawl and silver jewelry were never in doubt of the causes she championed so passionately and the honors she received:

- The first Native American recipient of the Presidential Medal of Freedom (1963)
  - Ladies' Home Journal selection of Woman of the Year (1976)
  - Legendary Mother of the Navajo Nation (1984)

Annie Wauneka, mother of four daughters and five sons, is celebrated as the most honored Navajo in history.

Annie Wauneka,
proud, Navajo woman
clad in silver, turquoise and velvet,
standing with authority
and dignity
amongst the male elders
of the Tribal Council,
expounding a myriad of issues
to improve the health,
education, and well-being
of your people!
Ah, strong Navajo woman,
you became
"Legendary Mother"
of your people
as you tirelessly campaigned
to free them
from endemic poverty, sickness,
and despair.

You never forgot the horror
you saw in childhood—
the dying of thousands
of your people
all around you—
struck with an epidemic of flu
and possessing no resistance
to its ravages.
Nor could you forget
the devastation wreaked
on your classmates in school
by the eye disease—trachoma.
The suffering and dying
marked you forever.
You carried it within you,
deep in your soul, Annie.
It was the seeding of your future self
as you grew into adulthood,
observing all the while
the entrenched poverty
of your tribe.
You listened to your father—
a wise, respected elder
and Tribal Chairman of the Navajo.
He passed on to you
his wisdom
and his qualities of leadership,
like a straight rope of integrity
that remained firm

and upright
in spite of life's struggles.
He emphasized to you
the value of education
and the importance of
political strategies
for the advancement
of your people:

"Never let my straight rope
fall to the ground,"
he counseled.
And you listened
well and deeply, Annie.

You yourself rose
to leadership—
like a straight rope—
becoming the first female member
of the Navajo Tribal Council.
You made the connection
between poverty and disease,
campaigning for
adequate sanitation, better nutrition,
and clean water.
Armed with an education
in public health,
you fought tirelessly
for your people's well being.
As tuberculosis

devastated the reservations,
you battled against the causes,
demanding funds
for better living conditions and
medical care from tribal,
state, and federal authorities.

Ah, you were wise, Annie!
Your wisdom led you
to bring together
the traditional tribal medicine men
with modern Western doctors.
You interpreted and explained
to the people
the values
of both disciplines and practices
so that they would not fear
the strange new medicines
and so the doctors of the West
would come to recognize
the inherent healing qualities
of nature's herbs and plants.
Your dictionary
translating modern medical terminology
into Navajo
quelled the people's fears
and superstition.

Ah, Mother of the Tribe indeed!
You fed your people

with new life and hope,
healing woman!
Infant mortality fell
and deaths from disease declined
as they listened
to your teachings and advice.
You were not afraid, either, Annie,
to articulate the scourge
of alcoholism that ravaged
the Navajo.
You cajoled, critiqued, and pleaded
for abstinence and recovery!
Ah, mother of the Nation,
you rose like a goddess
in silver and turquoise
to heal and guide your people!

Even the infants
were blessed by your
mother-self as you campaigned
for infant swaddling clothes—
"layettes"
to protect them from the cold
and the scourge of pneumonia.

Ah, mother of the Navajo!
Your lifetime of service
left a whole nation stronger,
prouder, healthier,
and educated!

You, who once declared:
"If you see something
that is not right,
you must do something about it,"
did far more
than "something"!
You simply never stopped
loving and serving
until your death in old age.

Your straight rope
never fell to the ground, Annie!
A life of love, indeed.

Blessed are you,
Annie Dodge Wauneka,
Tireless Mother of the Navajo.

Rachel Corrie
(1979–2003)

Rachel Corrie grew up in Olympia, Washington, and attended Capital High School and Evergreen State College. She refused to accept violence as a reality, although the news media promulgated it by spending unlimited time and resources. She joined the Olympia Movement for Justice and Peace and later the International Solidarity Movement (ISM). Founded in 2001, the ISM is a worldwide movement open to individuals who are determined to end Israel's presence in the West Bank through nonviolent means. The movement's mission is to prevent the occupation of Palestinian lands by violating curfews, removing roadblocks that isolate Palestinian villages, and blocking military vehicles from destroying property and homes.

Rachel was drawn to the ISM movement and went to Rafah in the Gaza Strip in 2003. She was trained in the ways of nonviolent resistance for two days and was deeply distraught by what she observed. In her journals, letters, and e-mails to her family she recorded the destruction she beheld—the plight of the people, many of whom were detained or killed, and the unimaginable horrors all around her. Despite the violence that blanketed the region, Rachel focused on the overwhelming sense of gratitude and kindness she received from the people. They who had little or nothing shared life and love with her.

Her short-lived life in the Gaza Strip (a mere two months) left a lasting mark on those who met this passionate young woman. Horror gripped those who witnessed a U.S.-made, Israeli-manned bulldozer (a U.S. taxpayer gift to Israel) run over Rachel twice, crushing her skull and rib cage when she placed herself in its path in front of a local home to prevent it from being demolished. Her selfless commitment to peace and nonviolence continue to be a powerful witness and legacy for all who struggle for justice and human rights.

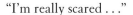

"I'm really scared . . ."

Not surprising, Rachel,
as you embraced the cause
of freedom
for the people of Palestine
and dared to leave family,
home, and country
to live in the midst
of a battle zone,
surrounded by tanks,
mortar shells,
and the terror of civilians.
What kind of madness was that?
At the age of 23
you had your whole life

before you—
all the dreams of the young
waiting to unfold
and delight you—
like seeds
gestating to burst.

It was a holy madness, Rachel!

But from your early teens
you knew and wrote of
a fire in your belly
as your awareness
of global violence, war,
and injustice
deepened and took root
in your very soul.
The passion you felt
would not allow you
to stay within
"the doll's house—the flower world"
that marked and blessed
your childhood.
You were consumed
by questions
that thrust you from
your small, young world
into the global arena
of human values and justice.
Our consumer society,

public apathy toward
hunger and poverty,
and wars—raging beyond
our safely guarded vision—
tore at your vision
for a world of peace and love.

So you stepped out
of your doll's house
and your flower world
clutching your dreams of nonviolence,
and burning with a passion
for justice,
you entered the war zone
of Palestine.

One young woman
driven by dreams of human dignity!
You were like the lamb—
daring to imagine
lying down with the lion.
You were David—
standing small and vulnerable
before a mighty armed Goliath.
You were believer—
dreaming a new Jerusalem
rising from the ruins of despair.

"I'm really scared . . ."

But the people welcomed you,
feeding you bread and tea
and receiving you
with love and hospitality
in their bullet-smattered homes,
amazed and awed
by the love and witness
of one frightened, heroic woman.
It doesn't take an army
to make a difference
or an impact—
just one transformed,
authentic person
refusing to buckle and flee
in the face of evil.

There you were, Rachel,
hoping that your
"international white person privilege"
would protect you
as you stood amongst
the people of Palestine—
your very presence
a defiant deterrent
against the tanks and the guns.

It is called solidarity.

Those without visions and dreams,
those whose eyes

have never shone with hope,
call it stupid and foolhardy.
So, indeed,
may be described all action
that propels
our earth-bound bodies
to heavenly spheres
where we can see—
ah, at last,
inching closer
on sweet distant horizons—
a new Jerusalem—
a place of peace and love where
"the wolf lives with the lamb
and the calf and the lion cub
feed together . . ." (Is 11:6)

Was it such a vision
that impelled you, Rachel,
to stand in solidarity
with the people
amongst their dead olive groves,
shattered greenhouses,
and bombed out gardens
and fruit trees?
Did such a vision
root you on the prophetic edge
where seers and saints balance
like holy acrobats
on the frail divide

between heaven and earth,
pointing with a passion
towards the possibilities
beyond our sight?

And was it such a possibility
that held you firm
before the bulldozer
as it roared to demolish
the Palestinian home
before which you stood
in vain protection—
one tiny human body
before a great steel monster?

One young woman,
dreamer,
prophet—
arms raised
like Jesus on the cross—
crushed and broken
like him,
by the sins of the world.

Blessed are you, Rachel—
brave and scared
sister of Jesus,
faithful daughter of God, and
young prophet for our time.

MOTHERS, SISTERS, DAUGHTERS

May your witness
and your martyrdom
inspire and give courage to us today
as we follow your footsteps,
walking the path
of peace and justice
that you bravely trod
before us.

Brigid of Kildare

(ca. 451–525)

Tradition has it that Brigid was born in Faughart, Ireland, the daughter of a pagan Druid chieftain (Dubhthach) and a Pictish Christian mother (Brocca). She was named after the Druid goddess Brig, the goddess of fire.

As she grew, Brigid became renowned for her generosity, hospitality, and charity—even giving away her father's precious jeweled sword to a beggar! Inspired by the teachings of St. Patrick, Brigid converted to Christianity. She decided to enter religious life—much to the displeasure of her Druid father. Brigid became Ireland's first nun and established a co-ed monastery of monks, nuns, and their children in Kildare in 470. Brigid brought together some elements of goddess worship into the Christian tradition. She was a bridge between the two great religious traditions.

Legend has it that Brigid was mistakenly consecrated a bishop by a bishop who claimed he was led by the Holy Spirit! For the Celts, Brigid, with her administrative and spiritual power along with her renown as healer and leader, was significant during their

transition from Celtic pagan spirituality to Christian religion.

Grounded firmly in Celtic goddess worship, Brig was also recognized as Christian saint and a powerful figure in Ireland's religious history. Her popularity was second only to that of Patrick.

Hail, Brigid of Kildare!
woman shrouded in myth,
mystery, and legend,
emerging now into our lives
from ancient Celtic times,
providing us with clues
and symbols
to piece together
our own Christian story.

Brigid, woman of two worlds,
born of a Christian mother
and a Druid pagan father
who named you Brigid
after the Celtic goddess, Brig.
Your soul was soaked in Brig,
the Great Mother,
whose name meant
fire—vigor—power.
Brig was protector of the land,
the crops, and the animals.
She was patron of women in childbirth
and celebrated Goddess of Fertility,

embracing all that lived and grew
on the rich green land of Eire.
Ah, Brigid, you were first
Daughter of the goddess,
she who was the guardian over
all your people and the livestock
on which they depended for survival.
The spirit of the goddess, Brig,
was celebrated
in groves and caves and hills,
in streams and wells
deemed holy and infused
with her healing power.
Nurtured by the cult of Brig,
you grew in goodness, charity,
and hospitality,
and came to be honored, Brigid,
for your care for the poor and
your kindness to all.
Until Patrick came
across the waters
with a new message for the Celtic people—
the message of Christ, Son of God,
born of Mary in a distant land.
And your soul, Brigid,
already full of virtue—
expectant and open to new possibilities,
embraced the new message—
the Good News of Jesus—
with the fire, vigor, and power

you had learned from Brig,
the Goddess of Fertility.

Converted by Patrick
you became the first Irish nun
and female Bishop
establishing your mixed monastery
of men, women, and children
in Kildare—
soon to become a center
of Christian pilgrimage and worship.
It was a time of transition
from Celtic spirituality
to Christian worship and ritual.
And you, Brigid, were the bridge.
The people honored in you
the spirit and virtues
of Brig the Goddess,
but named them now
the attributes and gifts
of Christian saint—
St. Brigid of Kildare.

We celebrate you, Brigid,
woman of God,
Christian saint and
daughter of the goddess.
We celebrate your fertility,
your receptivity, and your embracing
of all revelation

given to humanity
by the extravagant abundance
of divine grace
that knows no boundaries.
We celebrate
the fire of your love,
the vigor of your life,
and the power of your faith.

We pray, St. Brigid of Kildare,
that we too
may become vessels and bridges
of both old and new,
that we might bring together,
in tolerance and harmony,
different cultures, colors, genders,
religions, and nations
honoring the beauty and grace
of all creation
and proclaiming
the amazing diversity
of divine fertility.

Teach us,
Brigid of Kildare,
to open our minds and hearts,
wide and vast,
to embrace all
that Divine Love has created
for our delight.

The Syro-Phoenician Woman
(Mk 7:24-30 / Mt 15:21-28)

"Yes, Lord, yet even the dogs eat the crumbs that fall from their master's table." (Mt 15:27)

In the Gospels of Mark and Matthew we hear of Jesus' encounter with the Syro-Phoenician woman. Having been rejected by the scribes and pharisees, not understood by his own disciples, and even pressured by "his mother and brothers" to stop preaching, Jesus leaves his own territory and enters into Tyre and Sidon. We can assume that Jesus was seeking some respite and space to look at exactly what his mission was all about!

A Canaanite woman from that region approached Jesus. She is desperate, not for herself, but for her sick child. She shouts at Jesus: "Lord, have mercy on me! Lord, son of David, my daughter is tormented by a demon" (Mt 15:22). Exhausted, she has tried everything. She is a foreigner, an outcast, a woman. But she came

and knelt before Jesus begging for help. His initial response is rejection; the woman was not one of his own people and was considered low caste. Jesus is angry: "It is not fair to take the children's food and throw it to the dogs" (Mt 15: 25). (Gentiles were often called dogs by observant Jews—in first-century Palestine, dogs were not pets—they were wild scavengers roaming the land and eating whatever they could find.)

The Syro-Phoenician woman challenges Jesus who is taken aback by her response. Her comments about dogs at least getting crumbs from under the table put Jesus on the line in terms of mercy and compassion. Her daring works! Jesus responds as his understanding of his mission is stretched by the woman's challenge—the love and mercy of God is for all! The daughter of the social reject is healed, for great was her mother's faith!

I heard
about this man
whom they called
a prophet and a healer.
Some even called him Messiah!
Who cares?
The elites and the privileged
of this world can fantasize
and applaud and march
and proclaim
as much as they want.
I am too busy surviving
to be applauding,

proclaiming, or marching.
Ha! They wouldn't even want me
on their marches.
I don't fit, belong,
whatever.
They call me Syro-Phoenician.
In contemporary terms—
black or white trash
or loser.
Whatever.
Basically
I have no voice,
no rights, no name.
I live a world apart
from the man
they call prophet and healer.
Until one day,
I saw him.

He was out of place—
in my place—
my turf,
my territory.
What was he doing here,
in the hood,
the ghetto, the slums?

I knew it was him.
You could tell right off
that he didn't belong.

Anyone could see that.
He was out of place,
alien,
foreigner,
immigrant,
different.

But suddenly,
it didn't matter
what color or tribe or religion he was.
There was something more important
than all that,
I just knew it.
My heart began
to beat so fast . . .
until, unbidden,
tears flowed freely.

You see,
I had a baby,
such a beautiful baby—
only five years old.
She was sick,
ailing, dying.
My child,
my little one . . .
I watched her slipping away
before my eyes.
No medicine,
no care, no insurance . . .

I am desperate.

But he was there—
right in the midst
of my dying—
the stranger,
the foreigner,
the alien,
the immigrant
whom they called
prophet and healer.

And suddenly, it didn't matter
where he came from,
where he lived,
and whether he was
a foreigner and stranger.
Nor did it matter
where I came from,
where I lived,
and how poor I was.

All that mattered was
my child was dying!
And he was there!—
the one they called
prophet and healer!

I screamed aloud:
"Help me!

Come to me!
Listen to me!
My child is dying!"

He turned,
disturbed,
angry.

"Go away, woman!
You don't qualify,
you don't belong,
you're not included
in my group,
you are not chosen,
you have no rights.
Go away!"

I fell before him,
weeping for my baby,
weeping for mercy.

"Go away!" cried
the healer, the prophet,
"you are not included . . ."

And then my anger,
red as my anguish,
burst upon the hot sand
where I lay
sobbing in supplication:

"Even the dogs
beneath the table
get the crumbs!"
The man turned,
stiffened, transfixed,
as if struck
by a deep memory
suddenly breaking into
his consciousness
with an immense power:
"What did you say?" he mumbled.

"Even the dogs get the crumbs."

And then the man,
the prophet, the healer,
began to weep.
Right in front of me.

It was as if a long past memory
arose from deep within him,
seizing and touching him
in some mysterious connection.

He seemed, then, to see
and feel differently,
deeply, and
oh, so clearly!
"Woman," he said to me,
whispering gently,

"Woman, rise up.
Your daughter is made whole."

And in that moment,
in that glorious moment
of healing and new life,
neither he nor I
were foreigner, immigrant, stranger.

He was Son of God
who had recognized
and healed my child—
the daughter of God.

S. Matturco

Aung San Suu Kyi

(1945–)

A life lived for a cause deeply believed in describes Suu Kyi—
daughter, wife, mother, and political leader of Myanmar.
She was born in Rangoon, the capital of Myanmar (Burma) to
parents who were very active in the political life of their country.
Her father orchestrated Burma's independence but was assassinated when Suu Kyi was an infant. Her mother was the country's
ambassador to India.

Suu Kyi studied in India, England, and the United States and
earned degrees in philosophy, economics, and politics. Her political and educational interests did not diminish her family commitments. She was devoted to her husband, Dr. Michael Aris, a schol-
ar of Tibetan culture, and to her two young children, Alexander
and Kim. When her mother in Myanmar fell gravely ill, Suu Kyi
left her home and work in England to return to her homeland to
care for her mother. She was never to return.

Political unrest abounded in Myanmar and Suu Kyi was soon
drawn to support her people in their demand for democracy and
freedom. She witnessed the violent treatment and killing of peace-

ful protestors whom she joined under the banner of the National League for Democracy. She quickly became a threat to the ruling junta, and her calls for freedom and political reform led to her house arrest. After a six-year confinement she was offered freedom, but refused to leave the country, knowing that if she did, she would never be allowed to return. In 2003 she was arrested and imprisoned.

Appeals for her freedom from the international community and religious leaders were ignored, as was the request for a visa that would allow her husband, Michael, who was dying of cancer, to visit her and say goodbye. Separation from Michael and her children was a source of deep heartache for Suu Kyi. Eventually, in 2010, she was released. She has received numerous international awards, including the Nobel Peace Prize, and continues to campaign for her people's freedom.

Suu Kyi—
your photo
is clasped and revered,
kissed and stroked
like a lost, favored child,
by peasants, cab drivers,
farmers, politicians, and thousands
of ordinary Burmese people.
They see
in your tiny face
a mighty proclamation
of hope and freedom

in the midst of a country
ruled by the iron fist
of a military junta.

Suu Kyi,
what kind of fate
thrust you from the genteel
 and intellectual lifestyle
of upscale Oxford in England
into the passionate dreams
and violent demonstrations
of a repressed
and desperate nation?
You gave up
a secure and safe existence
to follow a deeper
and more insistent call
than that of home and family.
You crossed the globe
to return to your shattered
homeland,
leaving behind
and thus losing everything
that most of the world desires—
the security and comfort
of home, career, and family—
traded for the cries
of millions seeking
political freedom
in their impoverished land.

You became their icon,
their hope for the future,
Suu Kyi,
and in grateful awe
they called you
The Lady.

You stood—
a little wisp of life—
with flowers in your hair
in nonviolent resistance
before the mighty generals
with their guns, batons, and
rows of medals.
Another David before Goliath.

You faced the rows of loaded guns
with a strength
pulsing from within
a heart of steel
forged in goodness,
more powerful than any rifles
or rows of medals.

So they locked you up.
For years they
hid you away
to keep you from igniting
the fire of freedom
in the hearts of your people.

But they could not quench
the spark that burnt
deep and steady in you
behind your prison walls.
And they could not destroy
the longing for justice
in the eyes
of the ordinary folks
who waited and watched
outside those walls,
fiercely clasping their dreams.

How could
such persistent strength exist
in a tiny, graceful woman
worn down by imprisonment,
hunger, and ill health?
But you never wavered, Suu Kyi.
You never lost
your noble vision
for peace, reconciliation,
and kindness
in your brutalized homeland.

You never stopped hoping—
even in your years of
great loneliness and isolation.
Your hidden presence
lived and breathed
in the pulse of your people.

Did you dream of England—
of the gentle, green hills and
the peaceful flowing rivers?
Did you imagine holding again,
your husband and children?
Did you remember
all the picnics in the park?
And then, did you remind yourself
again and again
that freedom is the birthright
of us all—
holding precedence
over husband, children,
and picnics in the park?

Ah, you carried in your small frame,
Suu Kyi,
a huge weight of moral courage
as if you were a giant.

You did not permit
the flowers in your hair
to wilt,
Suu Kyi.
You replaced them daily—
ever fresh and lovely—
perfumed symbols, perhaps
to remind you
in your bleak and silent confinement

of beauty and perfection
and the potential
of the human spirit
through endless dreaming.
May your great courage
stir in us, Suu Kyi,
a consciousness of our own call
to stand before oppression and violence
with dignity and determination,
and—maybe—
flowers in our hair.

Sister Karen Klimczak

(1943–2006)

"A clown of God."

Karen Klimczak, SSJ, was born in Lackawanna, New York, the seventh of twelve children. Her father, a steelworker, labored hard and together with his wife spent time with his children inculcating in them religious values and providing the role models that eventually led Karen to a life of charity and grace.

Karen was an excellent student who excelled even as a young girl. After graduation from high school, she became a novice with the Franciscan Sisters of St. Joseph. She taught at Most Precious Blood School in Angola, New York, after completing her associate's degree from Immaculata College, today known as Hilbert College. She earned her bachelor's degree in education from Westfield State College in Massachusetts while she taught at St. Stanislaus School in Chicopee. After a fire damaged the school, Karen labored on behalf of the children's needs and redesigned the new school in the open-classroom learning style, the first in the area.

While pursuing her graduate work at Loyola University in Chicago, she joined ANAWIM (Hebrew: 'the remnants of society'), which was a liturgical performing arts company on campus. It was here that she learned the art of clowning. Transforming other's lives as well as her own, she created her own character, BOUNCE. Each letter a peace print into Karen's journey.

B — Be yourself; Be Truthful

O — Others and How We Should Act Towards Others

U — Use the Gifts God Has Given You

N — Never Hurt Anyone

C — Be a Caring Person

E — Everyone Is Special

In 1979, Karen transferred to the Sisters of St. Joseph in Buffalo, New York, because she was drawn to its charism of "unity and reconciliation"—"giving another a second chance." Her life of prayer led her, and she established a halfway house for ex-offenders. HOPE House ("Home of Positive Experience") was opened to residents, families, and guests. This house stood as a tribute to her parents, who had taught her to help "all" people who were in need. In 1991, Karen left the classroom and devoted her "all" to HOPE House Ministry. She believed, beyond words, that every person was special.

On a Good Friday afternoon in 2006, she joined others in downtown Buffalo to pray the Stations of the Cross. She returned to her home later that evening, surprising an intruder (Craig Lynch, a new resident of HOPE House) attempting to steal a cell phone for drug money. Startled, the intruder murdered Karen, removed her body, and buried it in a hole in the dirt floor of a shed. Authorities, family, and friends searched for Sister Karen for days. On Easter Monday Lynch confessed, and

Karen's body was brought out of the darkness of her tomb into
the light of Easter.

A martyr of love for "all" people.

Sr. Karen,
you loved the unlovable—
the kind of men
that the world resents and fears.
Men who are violent,
Angry, and destructive.
That's why they are locked up—
so the rest of us
will feel safe.

But you took them in, Karen.
You opened your door and heart
like a mother would
when her prodigal sons
came knocking.
You set up house for them
so they would have family,
warmth, and a home.
Whatever they had done
was irrelevant—dissolved,
forgotten,
in your passion for forgiveness
and nonviolence.
Described once as

"a little peanut of a woman,"
your vast heart,
with its amazing capacity to love
without reserve,
welcomed the violent
in a passionate belief
that healing was possible,
no matter what.
And so you stood in all the places—
on the bloodied sidewalks
and alleys
of your city streets—
praying for the victims
and their broken families
and even
(God forbid—in our vengeful world—)
for the killers,
gathering them in your mother-arms
to begin again—and again:
"Father forgive them,
for they know not what they do . . ."
Forgiveness was the force
that led you
to confront evil
with radical reconciliation—
the birthplace of hope.
Imagine, Karen,
oh, imagine our world
if we all were driven
by such impossible dreams

and visions
to work miracles!

"She hit me in the heart!"
declared one offender.
That's what peace does—
in our warring world,
it hits you in the heart.
It was your heart,
so filled with dreams, Karen,
that set you pinning
paper doves on telephone poles,
on trees, and all around the streets
where lives had been taken.
Your Peace Vigils shone
with burning candles,
lighting up the night
and the souls of those who
gathered round in the darkness.

You were excited about God, Karen.
And God was excited about you.
The Holy One surely knows
the possibilities that passion
can bring forth.
Why wouldn't God be excited
and expectant,
little peanut of a woman,
as you stood
clutching your paper dove

and candle
on the cold bloodied streets?

Together you worked miracles
in the city,
leaving offenders, politicians,
local folks, neighbors, skeptics,
and even church-goers
quite aghast
at the shining witness of your work
and the breaking and softening
of the hearts of hardened men.
You never drew the line, Karen,
even when they let you down
and stole your stuff.
You simply forgave
and started over.
How poignant,
how deeply moving and devastating
that your own violent death
should reflect the Easter story
of the Christ you so loved
and followed.

It was Good Friday
that you surprised, in an act of theft,
one of your own—
a Judas in your home
who turned on you
and killed you that awful Friday night.

For three days
your body lay in the tomb—
a make-shift hole—
while a city searched—
then, in numbed pain,
grieved the sudden quenching
of your light.
But rising above all the grief
and the horror and anger,
your words of forgiveness
were read aloud above the weeping:
"I forgive you
for what you have done.
I will always watch over you."
And the crowds of mourners were
stunned into silence before
the power and impact of
Compassion.

The people who walked in darkness
saw a great light
shining
from a little peanut of a woman.
And they were comforted
by its brilliance . . .

May your light shine in us now, Karen,
may we follow the Peace Footprints
that you so bravely
trod before us.

Blessed.
Blessed are you, Karen,
Woman of Peace.

Brenda Myers Powell

(1957–)

Brenda Myers Powell was born in one of the poorest ghettos of Chicago, Illinois, in 1957. She was the only child of a teenage mother who died within months of her daughter's birth. Brenda's childhood was violent. She was first molested at the age of four and continued to suffer sexual and physical abuse throughout her childhood. She left home at fourteen and began a lifestyle of prostitution that continued—spiraling into increasing violence and drug use—for twenty-four years.

Having effectively "hit bottom," she reached out for help in 1997 and moved into the Recovery Program that I (the author) was running in Chicago. Brenda embraced the road to recovery with gratitude and enthusiasm. Her passion and humor were contagious, and she became a well-loved and respected member of our small household—as well as my unofficial adopted daughter.

Brenda's passionate commitment to help women and girls leave the lifestyle of prostitution has led to her extensive involvement in recovery and anti-trafficking programs. She is a tireless

advocate against the sex trade and a member of the Cook County Sheriff's Department Prostitution Intervention Team. She is also co-founder of *The Dreamcatcher*—a not-for-profit foundation to help young girls stay out of the sex trade. Brenda gives talks on this issue all over the United States and has been featured in national magazines, newspapers, TV, and radio.

She claims that on her journey of recovery she stood on my shoulders. Now many girls and women stand on her shoulders—the journey continues!

~

The young teen
stood with fake posture outside
the run-down hotel,
watching the traffic
that slowed down to eye her—
up and down, inside, outside,
and beneath.
Dressed in lime green hot pant suit
and patent leather boots,
the child had no idea
that this was just the beginning
of a life of violence and brutality
that would span
her next twenty-four years.

There was no fond memory
of her childhood—
playing with dolls or toys—

only of being played with
by male adults,
drunk and groping for sex
with a four-year-old.
It went on and on . . .
It was normal for her.
It simply happened
all the time.
It was what men did
to little girls.

At fourteen she gave birth,
followed, barely a year later,
by a second baby.
Children bearing children . . .
It never occurred to her
that this was not the way
it was supposed to be.
It was, after all,
all she knew.
She also came to know
that she was beautiful.
Men lusted after her.
Even when she found a job
as a salesgirl,
the boss offered her
"extra work"—after hours.
Now she knew
it did not have to be
for free and,

anxious to provide
for her daughters,
she began a life of prostitution.
Then followed years—
marked by a dizzying and endless
parade of men
in dozens of states:
New York, California, Alaska, Ohio,
Louisiana, Mississippi, and more . . .

Her clients were business men,
politicians, entertainers, boxers,
drug dealers, celebrities, pimps,
gangsters, thieves, and
dignitaries.
They called her "Breezy"
for the skill and speed
with which she moved
from man to man.
She had no time to think
in the whirlwind of excitement,
glitter, and violence.
But, occasionally,
she had time to feel—
the sting of the slaps,
the pain of the bruises,
and the cuts from the knives.

But the mindless journey continued
as she moved

from street to street,
brothel to club,
hotel to motel, and
state to state,
dressed in furs and satin
with shining eyes
and flashing smile
belying inner horror,
devastation,
and ever deepening despair.

Drugs destroyed
consciousness,
providing blissful
but temporary stupor,
alleviating any awareness
of reality.
Even the beatings
were muted
by the power of crack cocaine.

Baby number three was born
jaundiced and shuddering
with drugs.
The tiny infant
was taken to a safer place
to be reared by a new,
responsible,
mother.

Taking refuge in a nearby shelter
Breezy huddled in the broom closet—
her own personal tomb—
for three long days
and nights
forgotten by the stressed-out staff.
Broken and sobbing,
no longer numbed by drugs,
she prayed to God
and to the baby
for forgiveness.

It was the breakthrough.
From despair, to defeat,
to surrender—
now all emptied out,
she found her way home,
longing to be filled
by the love of her children,
so long abandoned.
It was the beginning
of healing,
of miracles,
of hope.
She took the hand offered her
to turn around,
and she embarked on her journey
out of hell.
She staggered from drunken stupor
into sobriety

and began to see again.
She embraced the steep steps
of the recovery process
and began to live again.
She rose from dark dying
into a bright light.
And in that light,
"Breezy" died.
And Brenda Jean was born again.

And all who met her
would know it.
And all those who were trafficked,
abused, prostituted, and beaten
would come to know
that Brenda Jean was there
to tell them—
in clear, ringing and powerful voice—
that there is life,
there is hope
down there in that darkness.
Rising like the phoenix,
she stood now,
beautiful and radiant
with outstretched arms:

Come, sister,
Come.
Take my hand . . .
And, standing on her shoulders,
they do.

Rachel Weeping for Her Children

An endless flow of tears...that is what we know of this woman. Rachel showers the scriptures . . . We first learn of her in Genesis (Old Testament). She is the wife of Jacob—the woman whom he loved as much as he loved his own heart. He was exiled for seven years and served yet another seven. In spite of loving Rachel, he first married her sister Leah, who bore him offspring. When Rachel entered Jacob's tent for the first time, he thought "now sunshine has entered" but she remained childless. Rachel believed that she was the woman whom Jacob had chosen—that she was the one whom he loved.

Many years of sorrow befell Rachel before "God heeded her and opened her womb. She conceived and bore a son," Joseph (Genesis 30:22-23). Her tears suddenly subsided as if a new spirit flowed through her as she hoped for a beautiful life, but this joy was short-lived. She dreamt of entering the Promised Land with "her" children, but Rachel, the first woman in scripture to die in

childbirth, remains before us as the mother in agony beholding her child. After the birth of her second son, her final words echo loudly: Ben-Oni (Son of Sorrow). Before her death, the floodgates in her eyes reopen—dreams and visions gone—her tears—how many? Too numerous to count. Her child's name Ben-Oni changed by her husband, Jacob, to Benjamin. Why?

Rachel's tears again surface in the prophet Jeremiah. How fitting that the prophet of tears recalls Rachel. In his songs of lamentation Jeremiah curses his own day of birth. He speaks of Rachel's tears: "A voice is heard in Ramah, lamentation and bitter weeping. Rachel is weeping for her children; she refuses to be comforted for her children, because they are no more" (Jeremiah 31:15).

The Gospel of Matthew is sprinkled with Rachel's' tears. For a third time in scripture her sorrow is referenced. "Then was fulfilled what had been spoken through the prophet Jeremiah" (Matthew 2:17). She mourns her children. She will not be comforted. Again, the refrain is repeated with Herod's order to murder the male children in Bethlehem—killed even suckling from the breast.

Rachel—the mother of Joseph and Benjamin,
Rachel—one of the (mothers) who established Israel,
Rachel—would not be comforted.

~

It all happened at once.
Totally unexpected
and really the usual
day-to-day stuff . . .
But its impact

this time round
wrenched and
wounded my soul.

First a newspaper article.
Then a story in a magazine.
Then a report on the radio.
Then a news brief on my computer.
One by one,
as if they had lined up
to destroy my gentle day
(or was it a grieving God
who lined them up?),
they broke into my consciousness
and shattered my serenity.
They were stories and bulletins—
all true—
of our children—
murdered, trafficked, raped,
or sent to war
across the globe.
There were facts, statistics,
even photos,
that crashed into my space
screaming:
"Look what is happening
all around you!"
The girls and young women in Mexico—
hundreds of them—
accosted, brutally killed,

their bodies dumped
on the outskirts of the city
where they worked
in factories
for 50 cents an hour.
Their dreams of a better life
now dead—
like them.

And I heard the words of Jeremiah,
the prophet
deep within me:

"A voice is heard in Ramah,
lamentations and bitter weeping,
Rachel is weeping for her children."

Then another report,
bruising my senses,
about the child soldiers of Chad,
Sudan, Yemen, Congo,
Burma, and others—
over 250,000 of them—
dressed in fatigues
instead of tee shirts and shorts.
Their slight young bodies
tensing beneath the weight
of their AFK's—
trained to shoot people dead
instead of balls into hoops.

And the words of Jeremiah,
the prophet,
rose again:

"A voice is heard in Ramah,
lamentations and bitter weeping,
Rachel is weeping for her children"

And then the article on trafficking—
the violent, cruel enslavement
of our children
to sexual predators
in the bars, brothels, and clubs
of all our major cities—
one of the fastest growing
and most lucrative industries
in the world.
What am I to do
in the face of such horrors
wreaked upon
our babies and our young?
What am I to do?

A voice is heard within me,
lamentations and bitter weeping,
Rachel is weeping for our children.

But, oh!,
the temptation to be numb!
the longing

not to know,
not to hear,
not to feel.
It is all too much.
The burden is too great . . .

Until we hear
the weeping
of the mothers,
the sisters,
the daughters . . .
Until our silence is shattered
by the lamentations of those
who refuse to be comforted.
Then we know
that we must stand
with Rachel
and with women
who lament beneath the Cross
all over the world.
The burden is not too great
when we carry it together.
We must cry aloud
until our weeping rises
above the city streets,
until it is heard
in the barren deserts and
echoes from hill to hill
in a great global wail,
stirring the sleepers to awaken,

making the deaf hear,
the blind see, and
the dumb speak.
First a newspaper article.
Then a story in a magazine.
Then a report on the radio.
Then a news brief on the TV . . .
But this time
the world was watching
and listening
in stunned disbelief
at the great tsunami of weeping
arising from the women of the world—
millions of mothers,
sisters,
daughters,
who will not be comforted
until there is

No more silence . . .
No more silence . . .

And the voice of Rachel in Ramah
is stilled
by our mothers,
our sisters, and our daughters.

Wangari Muta Maathai
(1940–2011)

"People often ask me what drives me . . . Perhaps the mor difficult question would be: What would it take to stop me?"

Such were the words of human rights activist and environmentalist Wangari Muta Maathai. Born in 1940 to a farming family in Nyeri, Kenya, she was attuned to a home life that taught her to "respect the soil and its bounty." From the time she was a young girl, Wangari did not fit the traditional role of a Kenyan woman who was expected to fetch water and gather firewood. Instead, her brother recognized her giftedness and interceded on her behalf with her parents to send her to school when she was seven years old. She excelled in her studies and in 1960 attended Mount Scholastica (Benedictine College) in Atchison, Kansas, on an academic scholarship. She earned a bachelor's degree in biology in 1964 and one year later, a master's degree in biological science from the University of Pittsburgh. During this time she was deeply affected by the Vietnam War, and as she witnessed the many protests and

demonstrations she came to appreciate that people had the "right" to speak out for their beliefs. She returned to Kenya with greater resolve, and in 1971, earned her doctorate degree in veterinary anatomy from the University of Nairobi.

Armed with a deep appreciation for "life," she enmeshed herself in Kenyan politics to secure a better future for African women. For years she fought untiringly for the people's right to grow crops for sustenance rather than for profit as dictated by the government. With the government's profit policy, good, nutrient-laden land was destroyed, livestock suffered, streams and drinking water disappeared. To save the environment, she proposed planting trees. So convinced that her goal had merit, she left her teaching position and founded the Green Belt Movement (GBM).

The government was threatened by her vision and mocked her, stating that only professionals who worked the forest were able to plant trees successfully. Their ridicule was overshadowed as over a period of thirty years more than thirty million trees were planted. Nurseries were built and operated by women and jobs flourished. Wangari planted the seeds of hope for women as they took control of their futures in areas of family planning, nutrition and leadership.

This mother of three never backed down—never let hope die. It was no wonder that when her husband divorced her he said that "she was too educated and too difficult to control." In due time, the political life in Kenya improved, and women began to participate in policy decision making. Wangari's battles to improve the life of African women led to her arrest and imprisonment, but did not dissuade her from seeking political office. Her resolve was rewarded when she won a seat in the National Assembly in 2002.

Wangari Muta Maathai's achievements were many:

She was the first black woman and the first environmentalist to win the Nobel Peace prize.

"I wasn't working on the issue of peace specifically. I was working toward peace."

She was the first woman in East or Central Africa to earn a PhD and hold a professorship.

She shaped Kenya's new Bill of Rights.

She represented Kenya at the 2005 United Nation Commission on the Status of Women.

She received the Goldman Environmental Prize, the Right Livelihood Award, and the United Nations African Prize for Leadership.

Wangari Muta Maathai—a woman of many firsts and recipient of numerous awards, but none as significant as the accolade that she is first in the hearts of millions of African women.

It all began with a fig tree—

ancient and gnarled—
growing at the edge of the forest.

Your mother told you,
as a child, Wangari,
that it must not be cut
even for firewood,
because, she insisted,
it was

"God's tree."
And so, you were in awe
of God's tree
and the clean, clear stream
that ran beside it—
a child's Garden of Eden—
instilling in you
from earliest years
a love and awe of the earth,
the trees,
and the waters
that gave them life.
All of it was, for you,
threaded through
with divinity,
like a stream of God,
connected to and enlivening
the natural world
in which you played.
You lived in wonder, Wangari!

But as you grew
you saw the dying of the land—
the deforestation of your
Garden of Eden
in favor of cash crops—
tea and coffee—
grown for commerce and profit.
Whilst the government stole
and raped the land,

the people became bereft
of water, firewood, and soil
to grow the local crops
that for centuries
had sustained them.

You became a warrior, Wangari!
You began to speak,
aloud and passionately,
about the betrayal
of our kinship and connection
with the land.
The men in power
laughed at you,
deriding your passion
and dismissing you as mad—
a disobedient "little woman"
who did not know her place
and dared to cross the line,
disgracing real womanhood
(which knows its place).

But you stood up straight
before the onslaughts, Wangari.
Driven by deep memories
of the fig tree
and the clear, running stream
with divine thread
running through.
Driven by your mother's counsel

to care for and honor the land.
Driven by your conviction
that if the trees
were not protected,
the land would turn to desert
and your people would dry up
like the rivers and the streams
that no longer ran and burbled
with divine thread
running through.

So you gathered the women—
the ones who grow the crops
to feed their families,
the ones who carry water
to cook and wash,
the ones
who now lamented
the dying of the land.
And you began to plant,
teaching the village women
to gather bags of soil
and place tiny seeds
in the warm red earth.

Over the years,
like magic forests,
the trees sprang up,
reaching towards the sky
as if in thanksgiving,

providing substance to the earth
and holding rain to enrich
the once parched soil.
Millions of trees grew
in once desert places.
And the women now knew
they could change the world,
and it had started with
a fig tree,
a mother, and
a daughter.

But it did not end
with trees, Wangari.
You could not separate
the rape of the land
from human rape—
that of human rights and freedom.
You spoke for political prisoners—
locked up for protesting
oppression and injustice
under a cruel dictatorship.

You gathered the women—again—
the mothers, sisters, daughters,
of those imprisoned or killed.
Camping in the city center,
you dared call for the release
of the detained
and the names of the dead.

Arrested, beaten, and imprisoned,
you suffered for your passion, Wangari.
But you rose up again,
like the trees
that now reached to the sky
as if in supplication.
You returned to stand
for freedom
with the mothers, sisters, daughters—
now warriors for justice.
Attacked and harassed,
the women refused to scatter,
standing strong and noble
like the newly grown forests.
And the crowds grew,
marching through the city streets
with a power and inner strength
that withstood shields, batons,
and guns
until the prisoners
were set free.

The women wept and sang,
for they knew
they had changed the world.
Like Miriam of old,
you had led them dancing, Wangari—
singing their songs
of freedom and new life,
planting seed of hope

for all generations.

Blessed are you,
Wangari Maathai,
holy warrior,
woman of the soil,
friend of the fig tree and
the running waters.
Blessed are you!

May we too plant seeds,
one at a time,
until we dance again
in the garden of Eden.